thewizerd
kolnameonnee
Kcool1234
Dr_Mad
DARK_BYTE
babaroga691
pampos761
KING-OLE
R3miix-ABBAS
Pippyspot
Zanna136
loop8382
lolzeyes
AKKI3149
TeenieTurner
harry69066
sakibrulz
Donnyk46
DeJaMo
AirRandol
th100
Bushra
Zukov
fahadz36
Justice52
Filip-Croatia/Filip
Mr.Miniclip2502
Miran

THIS BOOK BELONGS TO:

....

THE MINICLIP TEAM:

Rob
CEO / Co-founder

Alexander
Head of Games

Andreas
Freedom Fighter

Ben
Director of Web Development

Bryony
Community Manager

Glen
Games Programmer

Jamie
Quality Assurance Games Tester

Jane
Operation Team Lead

Kieran
PHP Developer

Niclas
Creative Director

Nuno
Mobile Game Developer

Raúl
Senior Artist

Rob L.
Game Development Manager

Tito
System Administrator

Ruth
UI Designer

Sergio
Director of Miniclip Portugal (Smartphone Development)

Therese
QA Manager

Xiaoman
Game Researcher

Pieter
Director of Advertising

Sylvia
Advertising Manager

Zaina
HR Officer

... AND 142 OTHERS ALL OVER THE WORLD

EGMONT

We bring stories to life

First published in Great Britain 2012 by Egmont UK Limited
The Yellow Building, 1 Nicholas Road, London W11 4AN

Editorial & Design by Shubrook Bros. Creative.

ISBN 978 1 4052 6568 3
53863/1
Printed in Italy

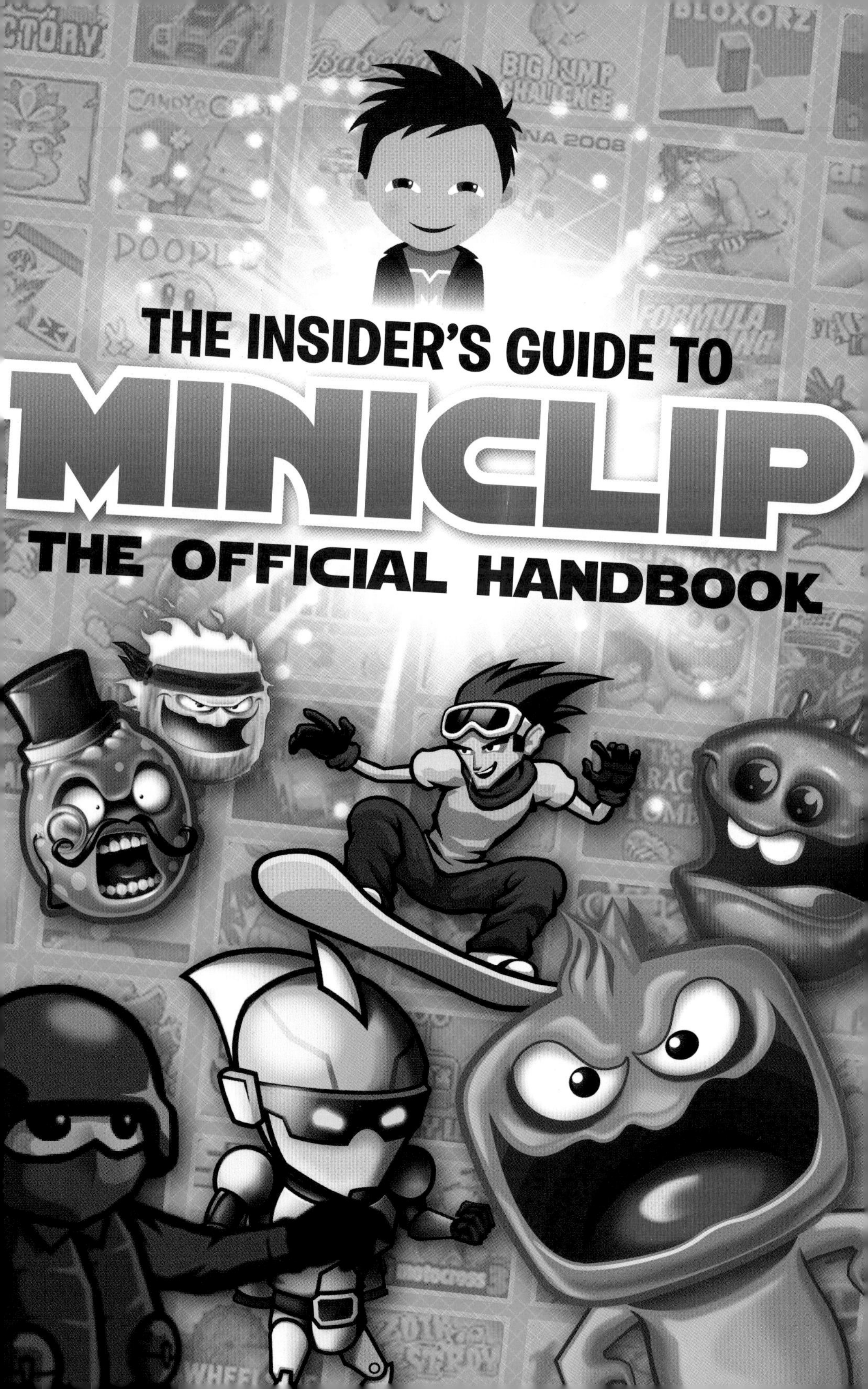
THE INSIDER'S GUIDE TO
MINICLIP
THE OFFICIAL HANDBOOK
BLOXORZ
BIG JUMP CHALLENGE

WHAT'S INSIDE?

Welcome! 6
Making Your YoMe 8
Action Games 12
Zoikz 14
MotherLoad 15
Dr Carter and the Cave of Despair ™ 16
Waffle Mania 17
Rubble Trouble Moscow 18
Base Jumping 20
Save the Sheriff 21
RoboKill 22
Wheels of Salvation ™ 23
Game Development 24
Develop Your Own Games 26
Sport Games 28
Free Running 30
Monkey Kick Off ™ 31
Cricket Defend The Wicket 32
China 2008 33
Urban Basketball 34
Extreme Pamplona 35
European Soccer Champions 36
Mountain Bike 38
Baseball 39
YoMe Celebrity Styles 40
3D Games 42
Rhino Rush 44
Saloon Brawl 45
Gas & Sand ™ 46
On The Run Vegas ™ 48
Age of Speed 2 50
War Copter ™ 51
Dogfight 52
Bow Master ™ 53
Awards 54
Multiplayer Games 58
RuneScape 60
Monkey Snowfight 62
OurWorld 63
5 In A Row 63
8 Ball Pool Multiplayer ™ 64
Goodgame Empire 66
Anagram Magic ™ 66
Boxo ™ 67
Sketch Star ™ 68
Games For Mobile & Tablet Devices .. 70

Puzzle And Strategy Games 72
Snow Line 2 74
Candy & Clyde ™ 75
Ice Temple 76
The Pharoah's Tomb 78
Mini Pets ™ 79
Sushi Go Round 80
Ice Breaker 81
Bloxorz 82
Bomba 83
Keeping Up With Miniclip 84

STUNT GAMES

Stunt Games 86
Extreme Skater ™ 88
Trial Bike Pro 89
iStunt 2 ™ 90
Stunt Pilot 2 92
TG Motocross 3 93
Gravity Guy ™ 94
Trials Mountain Heights 96

Developer Q&A 98

SEASONAL GAMES

Seasonal Games 100
Monkey Lander 102
Moby Dick 2 103
Acid Factory 104
Polar Jump 105
Skywire 2 106
Monster Island ™ 107
Snowball 108
Raft Wars 109
Doodle 2 110
Big Jump Challenge 111

Your Interactive Hub 112

MOTORSPORT GAMES

Motorsport Games 114
Monster Trucks Nitro 2 116
Superbike Race Off ™ 118
Agent: FreeRide Aqua Escape ™ 119
Motocross Country Fever 120
Formula Racing 122
Miniclip Rally ™ 123
Turbo Racing 2 124

Developer Q&A 126

SHOOT 'EM UP AND TOWER DEFENSE GAMES

Shoot 'em Up And Tower Defense Games 128
Hambo 130
Robo Rampage ™ 132
Fighter Pilot 2 133
Canyon Shooter 2 134
Heli Attack 3 135
Commando 3 ™ 136
Zombie Defense Agency 138
Canyon Defense 2 139

STAFF FAVES

Staff Faves 140
Joe Destructo ™ 142
Zombotron 143
Jousting 144
Disc Pool 145
Club Penguin 146
Amazing Sheriff 148
UFO Joe 149
Fragger: Lost City ™ 150

Your Tips 152
Developer Q&A 154
Your Gaming Journal 156
Game Index 158

WELCOME!

SO, CHECK IT OUT ...

Welcome to *The Insider's Guide to Miniclip*. For those of you who are out of the loop, Miniclip is a totally interactive social gaming site. You can compete against friends and in-game opponents or friends to earn awards. Plus, you can rank your scores on leaderboards and generally have the best gaming experience of your life! So, now that you're initiated, here it is ... a book completely dedicated to Miniclip. Let's fire up the homepage and get gaming!

CEO / Co-founder

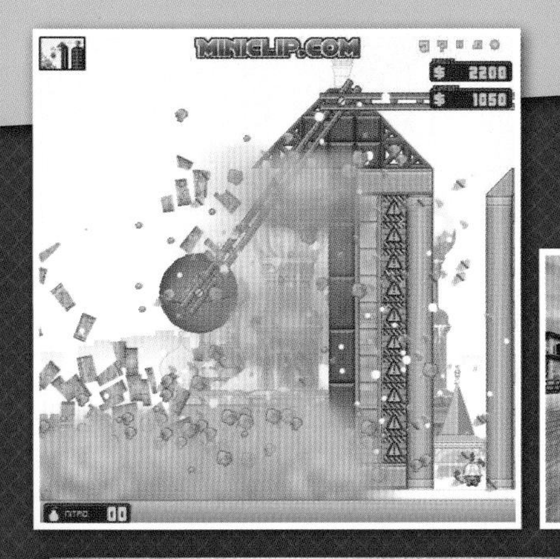

A GALAXY OF GAMES

Miniclip is more than just games – it's an experience. From the moment you create your avatar (known as a YoMe) to the first time you discover a game you just can't stop playing, our site is here to entertain you. Some games are funny, some are challenging and some are just plain crazy, but all are guaranteed to give you hours of fun. Let the games begin!

Meet the team ...
Miniclip is run by a dedicated team of rather unusual people. Keep an eye out for more about us later.

MAKING YOUR YOME

If you're a new user, head to the profile tab and begin creating your YoMe avatar! The first thing you'll have to do is decide if you're a boy or a girl! If you can't handle that decision, then maybe you should pop off the computer and have a lie down!

FEATURES

SKIN COLOUR ...

There are tons of skin colours to choose from. Take a look at your arm and choose the best colour for you.

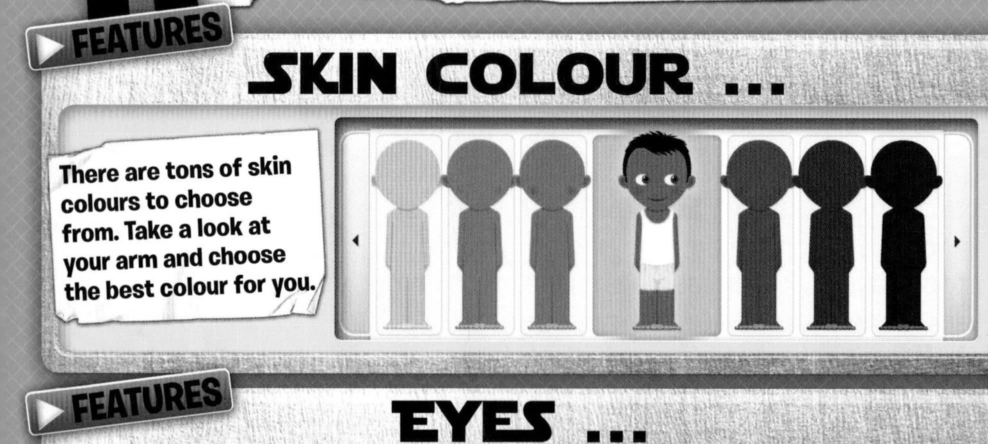

FEATURES

EYES ...

Ever fancied having different colour eyes? Now's your chance to change them!

FEATURES

MOUTH ...

Not only can you choose a mouth here, but you can go for a full face paint too! Love it!

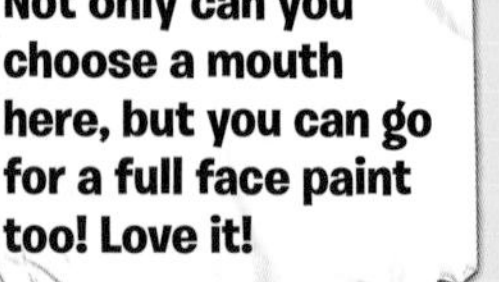

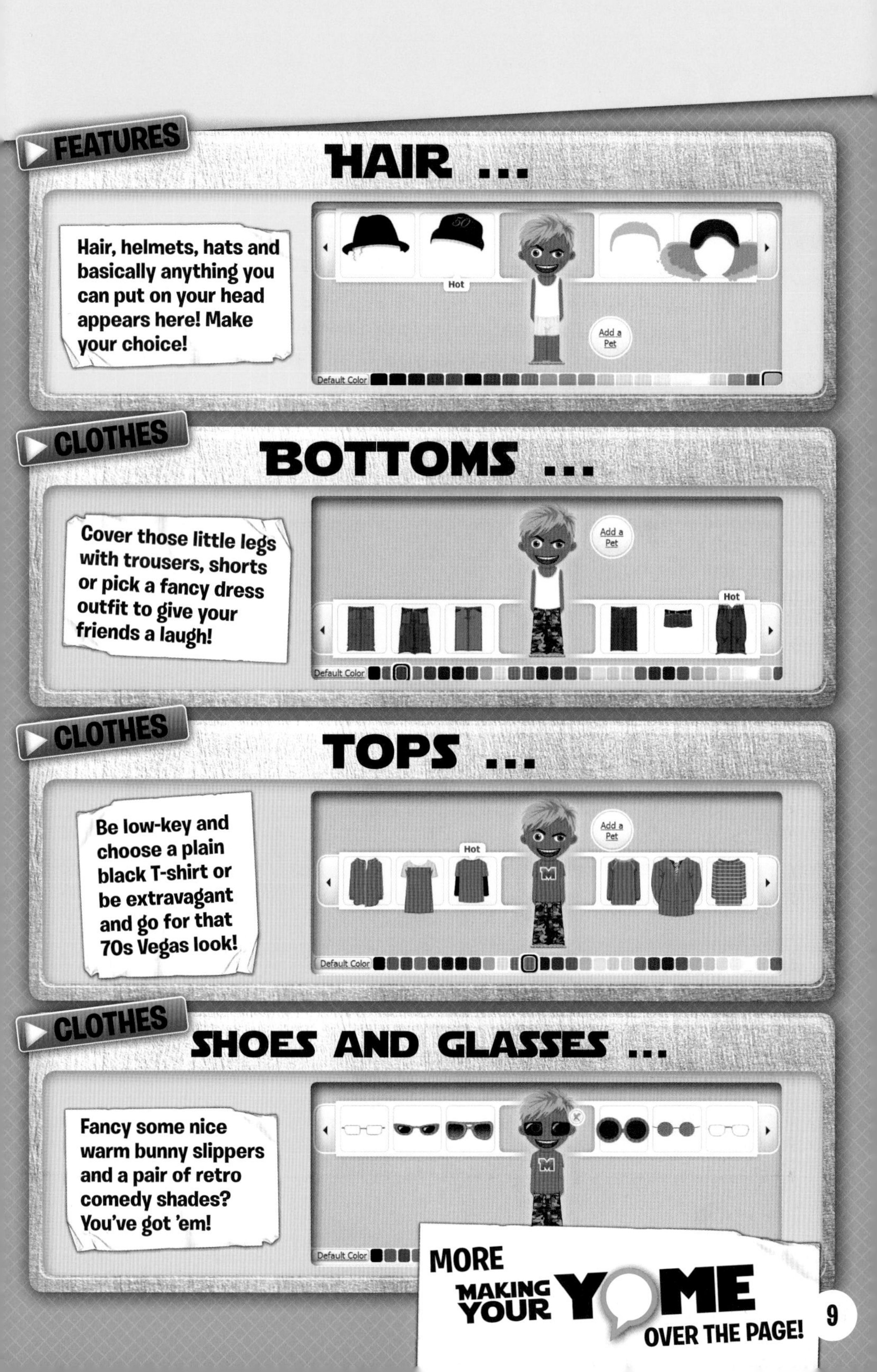
FEATURES
HAIR ...
Hair, helmets, hats and basically anything you can put on your head appears here! Make your choice!
Hot
Add a Pet
Default Color
CLOTHES
BOTTOMS ...
Cover those little legs with trousers, shorts or pick a fancy dress outfit to give your friends a laugh!
Add a Pet
Hot
Default Color
CLOTHES
TOPS ...
Be low-key and choose a plain black T-shirt or be extravagant and go for that 70s Vegas look!
Add a Pet
Hot
Default Color
CLOTHES
SHOES AND GLASSES ...
Fancy some nice warm bunny slippers and a pair of retro comedy shades? You've got 'em!
Default Color
MORE MAKING YOUR YOME OVER THE PAGE!

MAKING YOUR YOME

MY ROOM & PETS

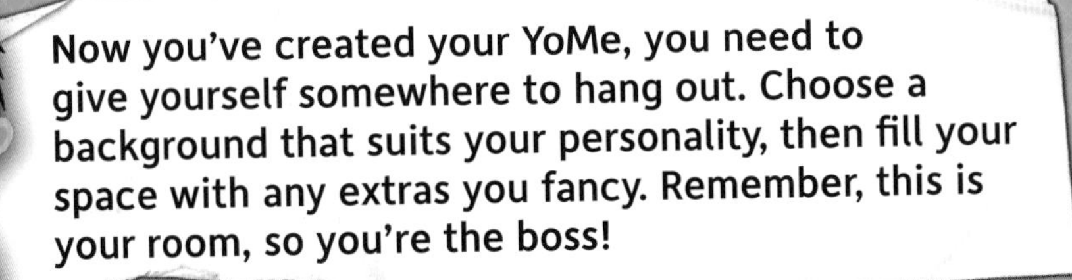

Now you've created your YoMe, you need to give yourself somewhere to hang out. Choose a background that suits your personality, then fill your space with any extras you fancy. Remember, this is your room, so you're the boss!

MY ROOM

BACKGROUND ...

Put yourself in a scene or just select a funky background to give your YoMe a place to hang out.

MY ROOM

EXTRAS ...

Whether you're into books, computers, pets or games, you can find plenty of extras to fill your room.

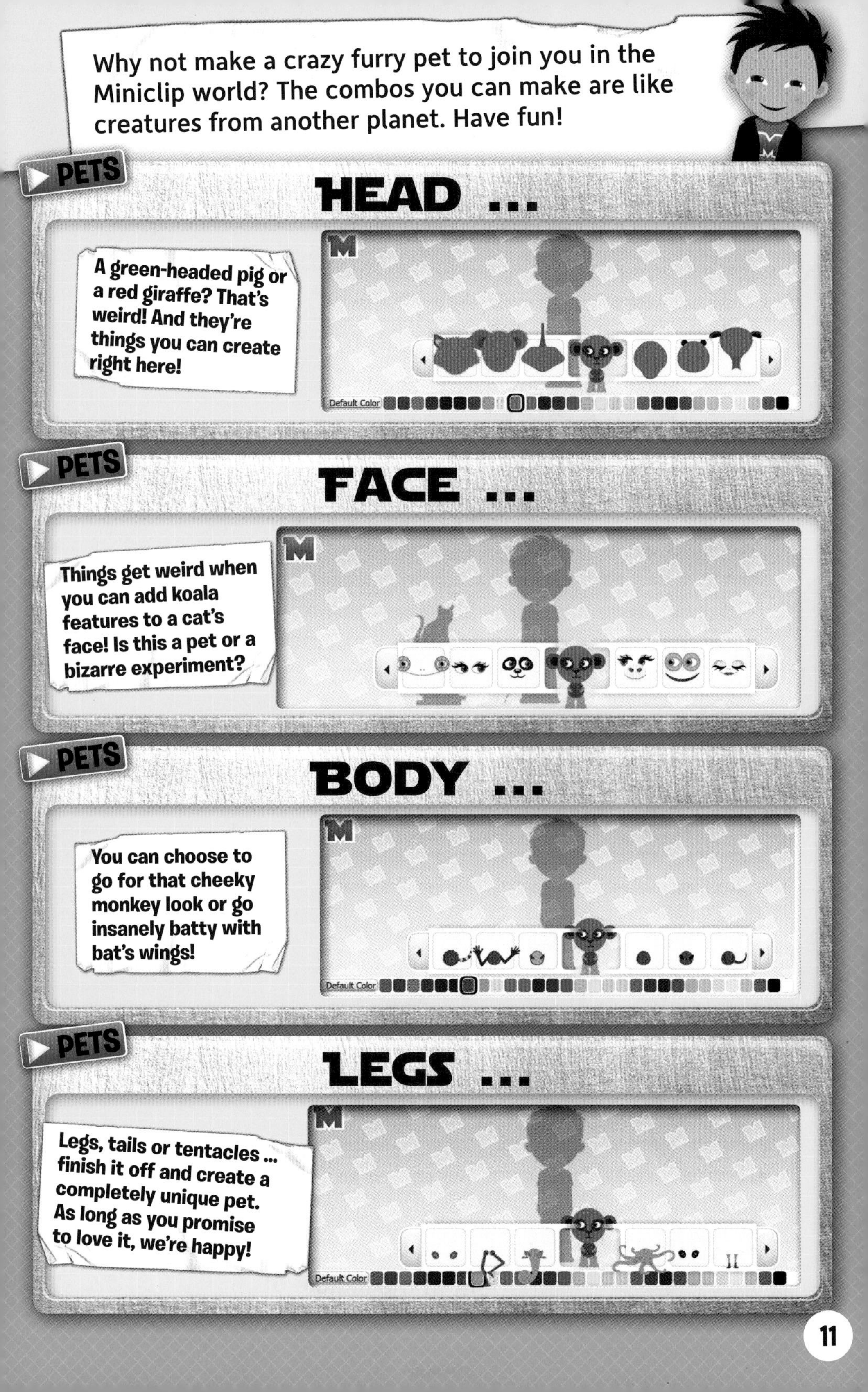

Why not make a crazy furry pet to join you in the Miniclip world? The combos you can make are like creatures from another planet. Have fun!
PETS
HEAD ...
A green-headed pig or a red giraffe? That's weird! And they're things you can create right here!
Default Color
PETS
FACE ...
Things get weird when you can add koala features to a cat's face! Is this a pet or a bizarre experiment?
PETS
BODY ...
You can choose to go for that cheeky monkey look or go insanely batty with bat's wings!
Default Color
PETS
LEGS ...
Legs, tails or tentacles ... finish it off and create a completely unique pet. As long as you promise to love it, we're happy!
Default Color

GLEN

PAGE 16

FAVE ACTION GAME:
CAVE OF DESPAIR

WHY? One of my favourite films is Indiana Jones! This game takes Dr Carter on similar adventures.

HIGH SCORE
2,884

RAÚL

PAGE 17

FAVE ACTION GAME:
WAFFLE MANIA

WHY? I love trying to stay on top of this game! It can get manic trying to keep up with the demanding customers.

HIGH SCORE
10,545

ROB

PAGE 18

FAVE ACTION GAME:
RUBBLE TROUBLE

WHY? Sometimes you just want to demolish stuff! The Rubble Trouble series is perfect for that.

HIGH SCORE
29,190

TITO

PAGE 22

FAVE ACTION GAME:
ROBOKILL

WHY? Sci-fi is one of my fave film genres and this awesome game puts me right in the middle of the action.

HIGH SCORE
LEVEL 8

ACTION GAMES

This zone is purely for the adrenaline junkie! There aren't many places you can have a Wild West brawl before breakfast, take down the enemy as a machine-gun-brandishing pig by lunchtime and prevent the outbreak of World War III before you go to bed. Luckily, you can do all that and more right here!

CHECK OUT A STACK OF INSANE ACTION GAMES

WHAT'S IT ABOUT?

Evil Zoikz are trying to overrun your computer! It's up to you to defend the mainframe by placing automatic mini-weapons around the circuits to destroy the Zoikz as they pass. Place your weapons carefully around the battle zone and upgrade by shooting the Zoikz. Choose your weapons wisely and good luck ... your computer needs you!

MINI TIP

LOOK OUT FOR THE CHEAT SHEETS AT THE END OF EACH GAME.

CONTROLS

PLACE MINI-WEAPONS

MY SCORES

High Score

....

RATE-O-METER

What do you think of Zoikz? Rate it by colouring the scale below.

Total Awesomeness!

Not my fave!

ROB'S TIP!

YOU CAN'T MOVE A WEAPON ONCE YOU'VE PLACED IT, SO THINK ABOUT IT FIRST!

EVIL ZOIKZ ARE TAKING OVER YOUR COMPUTER. STOP THEM IF YOU CAN!

GAMES IN THE SERIES

ZOIK AND DESTROY

In this game, the Zoikz are back and they're sneakier than ever. Seek and destroy the Zoikz hidden in each level before they zap the master CPU chip!

MOTHERLOAD

WHAT'S IT ABOUT?

Head to Mars and use your digger to excavate as many minerals as possible. Start off with a basic mining machine and upgrade your digger as you go. Spend the money you earn to buy supplies in the fully-computerised shops. It's your job to move deeper underground, collect those minerals and bring them back to the surface for processing.

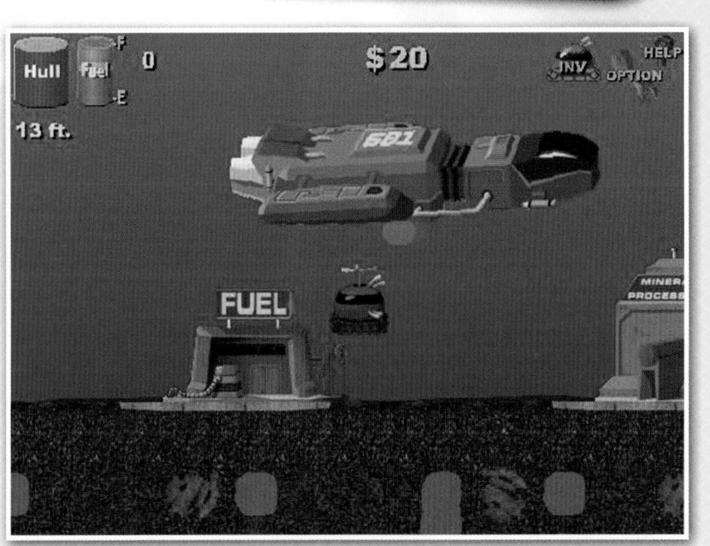

UNEARTH THE MYSTERIES BELOW THE SURFACE OF MARS!

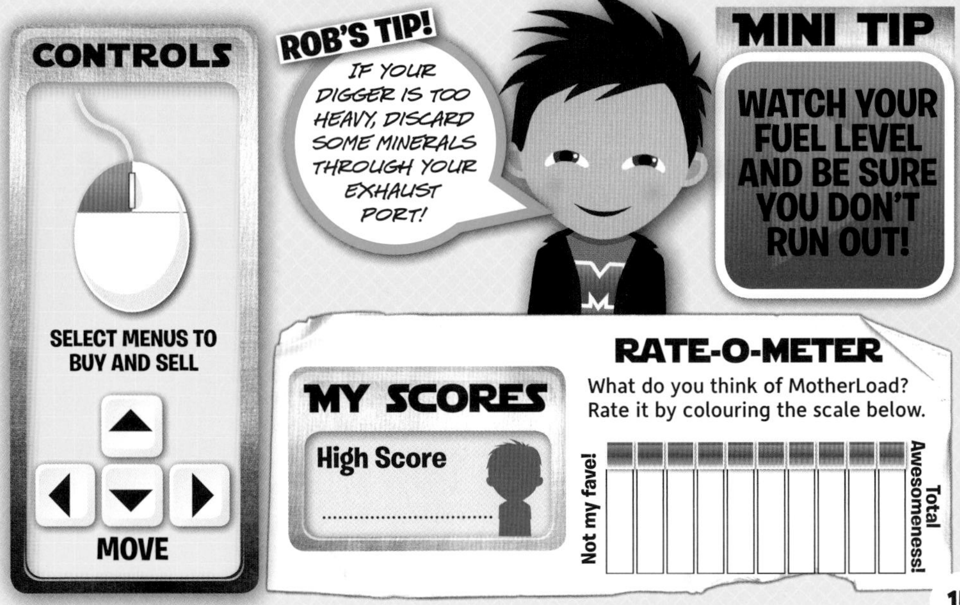

DR CARTER AND THE CAVE OF DESPAIR™

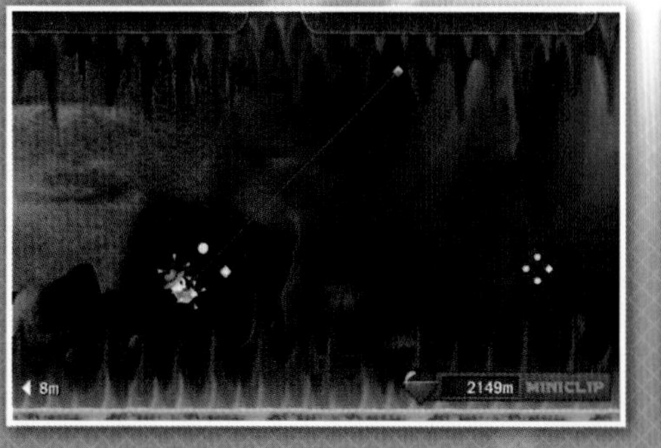

WHAT'S IT ABOUT?

Get ready for some hot bottom-burning action! Join Dr Carter and escape the wave of molten lava that's hurtling behind him at awesome speed. Swing his rope up to the rocky ceiling to catapult him through the deadly cave. Beware not to drop too low or the seat of his pants will get pretty scorched. Ouch!

CONTROLS

AIM

CLICK AND HOLD TO SWING ON YOUR WHIP. RELEASE TO LET GO.

GLEN'S TIP!

DON'T MAKE THE ROPE TOO LONG OR DR CARTER WILL SWING DOWN INTO THE LAVA.

MINI TIP

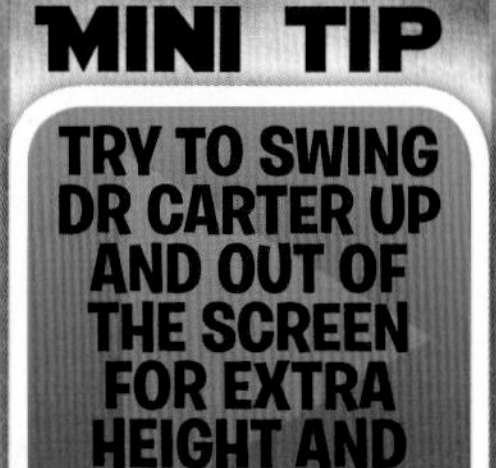

TRY TO SWING DR CARTER UP AND OUT OF THE SCREEN FOR EXTRA HEIGHT AND DISTANCE.

BEWARE NOT TO DROP TOO LOW OR DR CARTER'S PANTS WILL GET PRETTY SCORCHED!

MY SCORES

High Score

....

RATE-O-METER

What do you think of Dr. Carter and the Cave of Despair? Rate it by colouring the scale below.

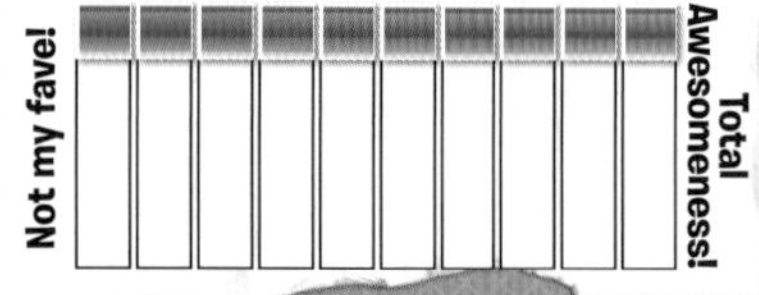

WHAT'S IT ABOUT?

Are you hungry? Are you hungry for **ice cream**? Then, you've come to the right place. The only thing is, here you'll be serving it ... not eating it! Your job is to keep your customers happy as they become more and more adventurous with their orders. Get the cups, get the ice cream, get the toppings and get gaming!

AWARDS

GOLD
Achieve Waffle Mania Gold award by getting a score of **9,000.**

RAÚL'S TIP!

YOUR CUSTOMERS ARE IMPORTANT. DON'T LET THEM WAIT TOO LONG... THEY GET ANGRY!

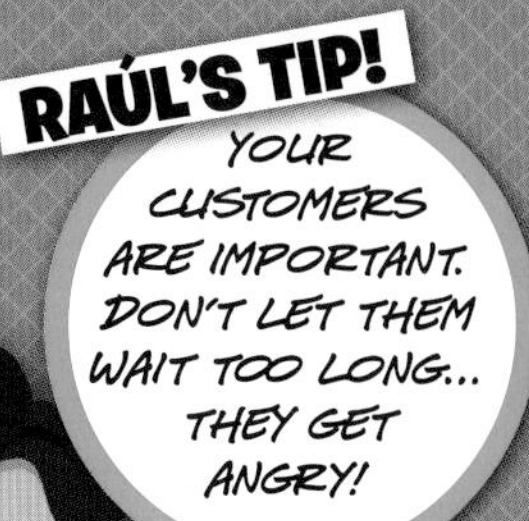

CONTROLS

SELECT THE CUP, ICE CREAM AND TOPPING, THEN SERVE.

MY SCORES

High Score

....

RATE-O-METER

What do you think of Waffle Mania? Rate it by colouring the scale below.

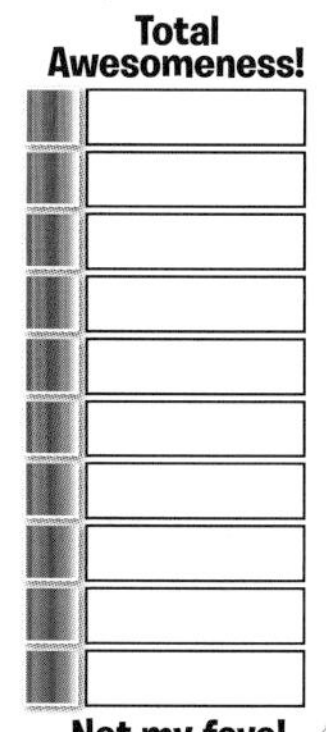

MINI TIP

IF AN ORDER GOES WRONG, TRASH THE ICE CREAM AND START AGAIN QUICKLY!

IF YOU'RE HUNGRY FOR ICE CREAM, THEN YOU'VE COME TO THE RIGHT PLACE.

RUBBLE TROUBLE MOSCOW

WHAT'S IT ABOUT?

These crazy guys just never stop blowing things up! Here, Rubble Trouble take their demolition addiction to the snowy venue of Moscow (that's in Russia). Things are hottin' up in the freezin' cold! Use explosives and deploy tanks to reduce buildings to piles of rubble to make some cash. Don't hang around on the job though – you don't want your engine to freeze! Keep moving – there's no time to chill!

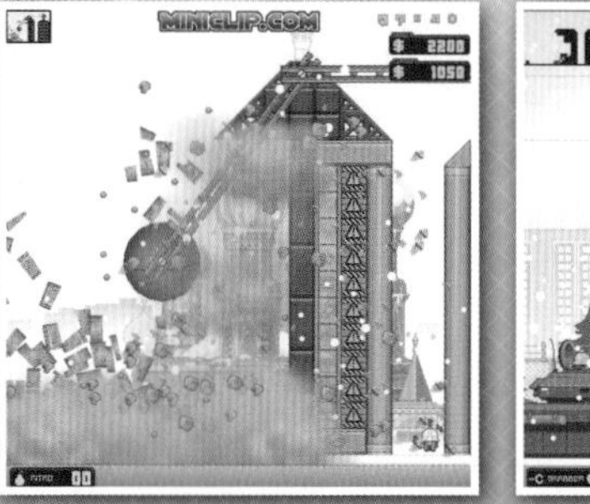

CONTROLS

SELECT YOUR DEMOLITION TOOL.
MOVE AND PLACE YOUR TOOL.

MINI TIP

THESE GUYS HAVE PLENTY TO SAY. MAKE SURE YOU READ THEIR TIPS.

AWARDS

GOLD

Reduce everything to ground level and score **100,000 points**. Oh, yeah ... watch out for the bears!

SILVER

Use all the demolition equipment creatively and score a total of **50,000 points**.

BRONZE

Travel to Moscow with the ultimate demolition crew and get wrecking to the tune of **25,000 points**.

RUBBLE TROUBLE

In a quiet city landscape, the Rubble Trouble team liven things up by reducing buildings to piles of rubble in the first incarnation of the Rubble Trouble games.

RUBBLE TROUBLE TOKYO

Rubble Trouble travel to Tokyo to do what they do best against the night skyline of the Japanese city.

ROB'S TIP!

ON LEVEL 6, DESTROY THE GIRDER FIRST AND THEN TAKE OUT THE PENDULUM.

MY SCORES

High Score

....

RATE-O-METER

What do you think of Rubble Trouble Moscow? Rate it by colouring the scale below.

Total Awesomeness!

Not my fave!

BASE JUMPING

WHAT'S IT ABOUT?

Base Jumping is one thing, but are you good enough to challenge the king? There's only one way to find out. Pit yourself against the best in the world and make your way through the leagues. Ironically, the best way to get to the top in this game is by jumping to the bottom ... fast! So get going and become the champ of extreme sports.

JUMP AGAINST THE BEST IN THE WORLD AND TOP THE LEAGUE.

AWARDS

GOLD
Become the Golden Base Jumper by getting **28,000 points**!

ROB'S TIP!

JUMP AS SOON AS YOU SEE THE WORD 'GO'. DON'T JUMP BEFORE OR YOU'LL BE DISQUALIFIED.

MY SCORES

High Score ....

RATE-O-METER

What do you think of Base Jumping? Rate it by colouring the scale below.

Total Awesomeness!

Not my fave!

CONTROLS

SPACE
JUMP / OPEN CHUTE

MINI TIP

DON'T LEAVE IT TOO LATE TO OPEN YOUR PARACHUTE ... YOU WON'T SURVIVE THE IMPACT!

SAVE THE SHERIFF

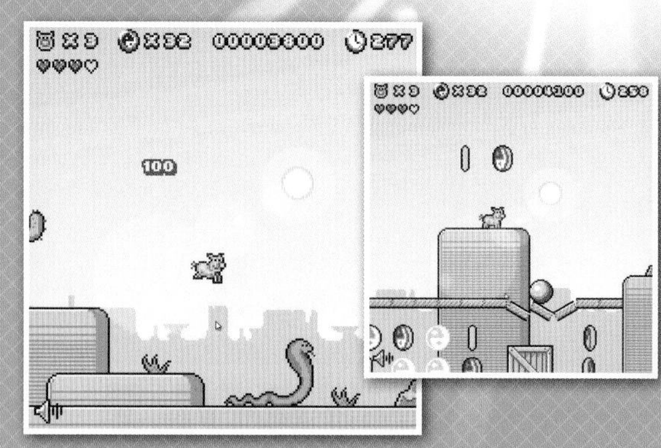

WHAT'S IT ABOUT?

Everyone loves the sheriff ... especially his trusty pig! It's down to you to help the pig collect the stolen coins dropped by the robbers as you search for your master. This Wild West adventure is full of snakes, frogs, fish and the highest jumping pig you've ever seen in your life! Yeehaw!

THIS WILD WEST ADVENTURE HAS THE HIGHEST-JUMPING PIG YOU'VE EVER SEEN!

ROB'S TIP!

YOU CAN USE THE CACTUSES AS LADDERS TO HELP YOU MOVE ONTO HIGHER PLATFORMS.

CONTROLS

- Arrow keys: MOVE
- SHIFT: HOLD TO REMOVE DIRT WITHOUT MOVING
- Q: QUIT
- P: PAUSE

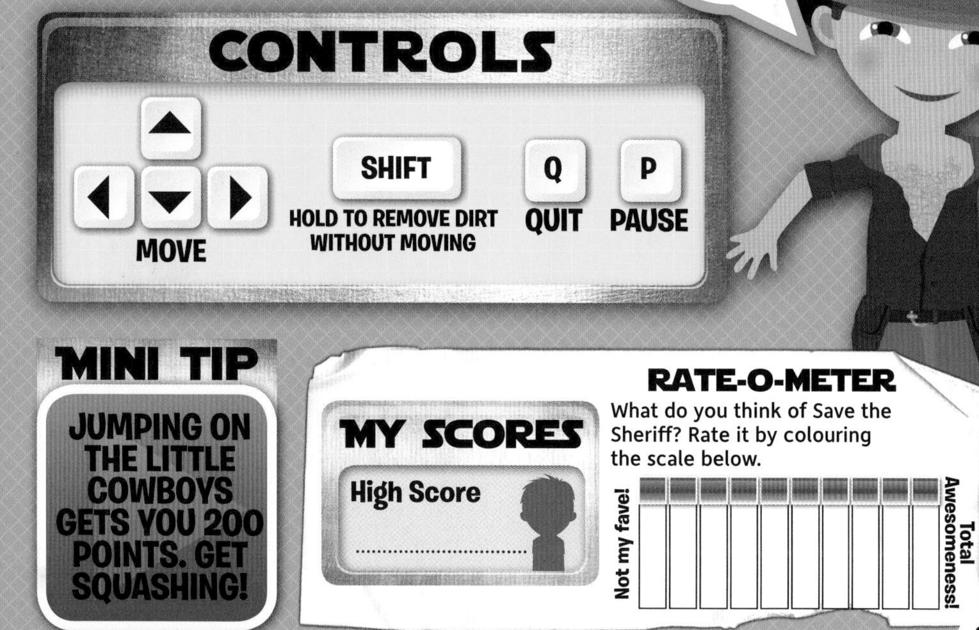

MINI TIP

JUMPING ON THE LITTLE COWBOYS GETS YOU 200 POINTS. GET SQUASHING!

MY SCORES

High Score ....

RATE-O-METER

What do you think of Save the Sheriff? Rate it by colouring the scale below.

Not my fave! — Total Awesomeness!

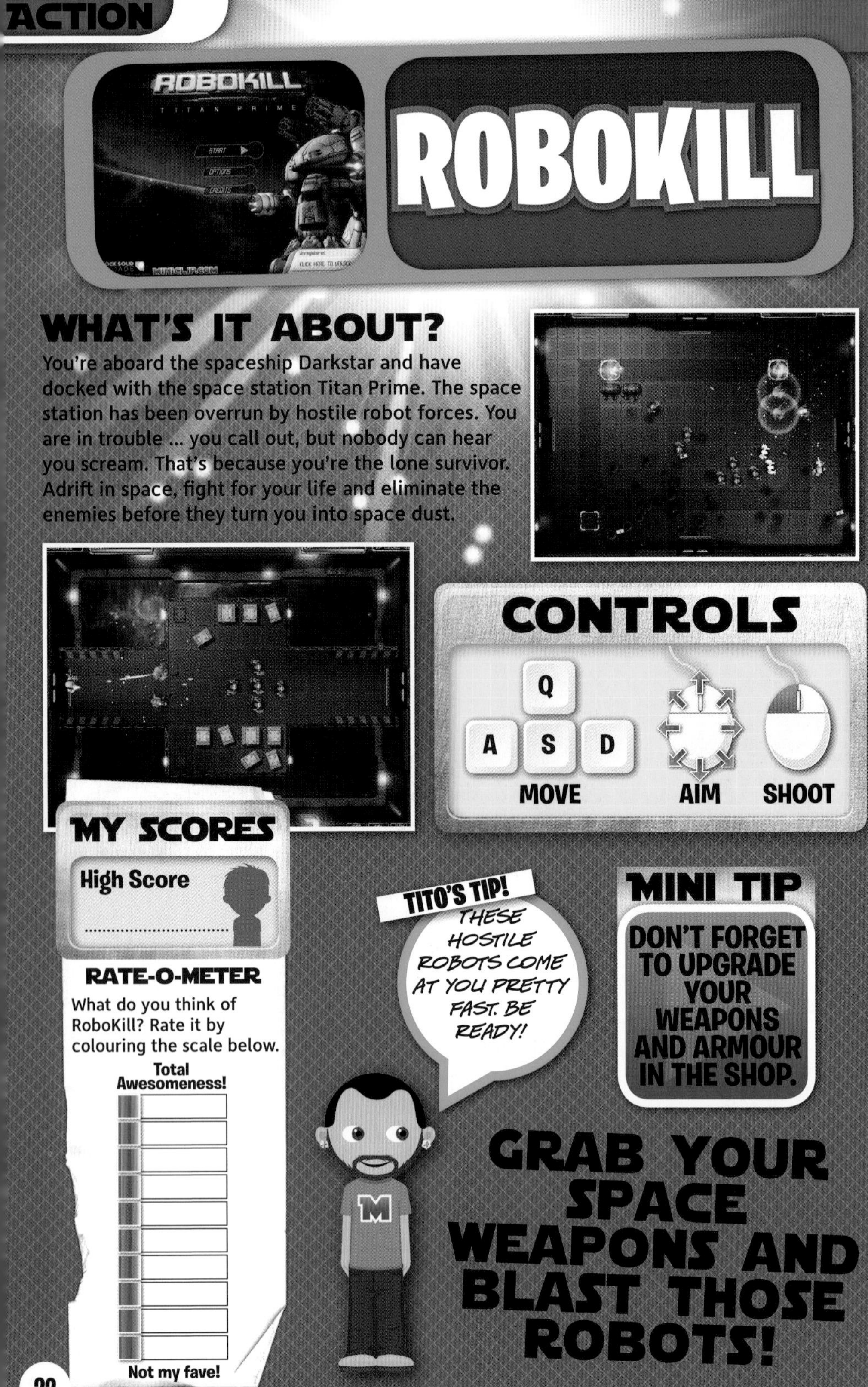

ROBOKILL

WHAT'S IT ABOUT?

You're aboard the spaceship Darkstar and have docked with the space station Titan Prime. The space station has been overrun by hostile robot forces. You are in trouble ... you call out, but nobody can hear you scream. That's because you're the lone survivor. Adrift in space, fight for your life and eliminate the enemies before they turn you into space dust.

CONTROLS

Q A S D – MOVE
AIM
SHOOT

MY SCORES

High Score ....

RATE-O-METER

What do you think of RoboKill? Rate it by colouring the scale below.

Total Awesomeness!

Not my fave!

TITO'S TIP!

THESE HOSTILE ROBOTS COME AT YOU PRETTY FAST. BE READY!

MINI TIP

DON'T FORGET TO UPGRADE YOUR WEAPONS AND ARMOUR IN THE SHOP.

GRAB YOUR SPACE WEAPONS AND BLAST THOSE ROBOTS!

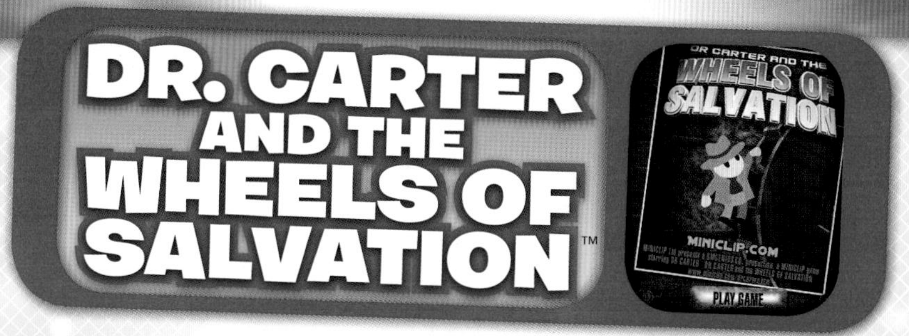

WHAT'S IT ABOUT?

Last we saw of Dr. Carter, he was escaping a wave of molten lava. Things don't get much easier for this adventurous explorer – he just loves underground danger! Here, you have to help him jump onto the ever-rotating wheels. Don't mess up or he'll plummet into the pit of Endless Torment – no pressure!

ROB'S TIP!
WATCH OUT FOR THE TINY WHEELS. THEY SEND DR CARTER SPINNING LIKE A PROPELLER!

DR CARTER JUST LOVES UNDERGROUND DANGER! THIS IS THE 'WHEEL' DEAL!

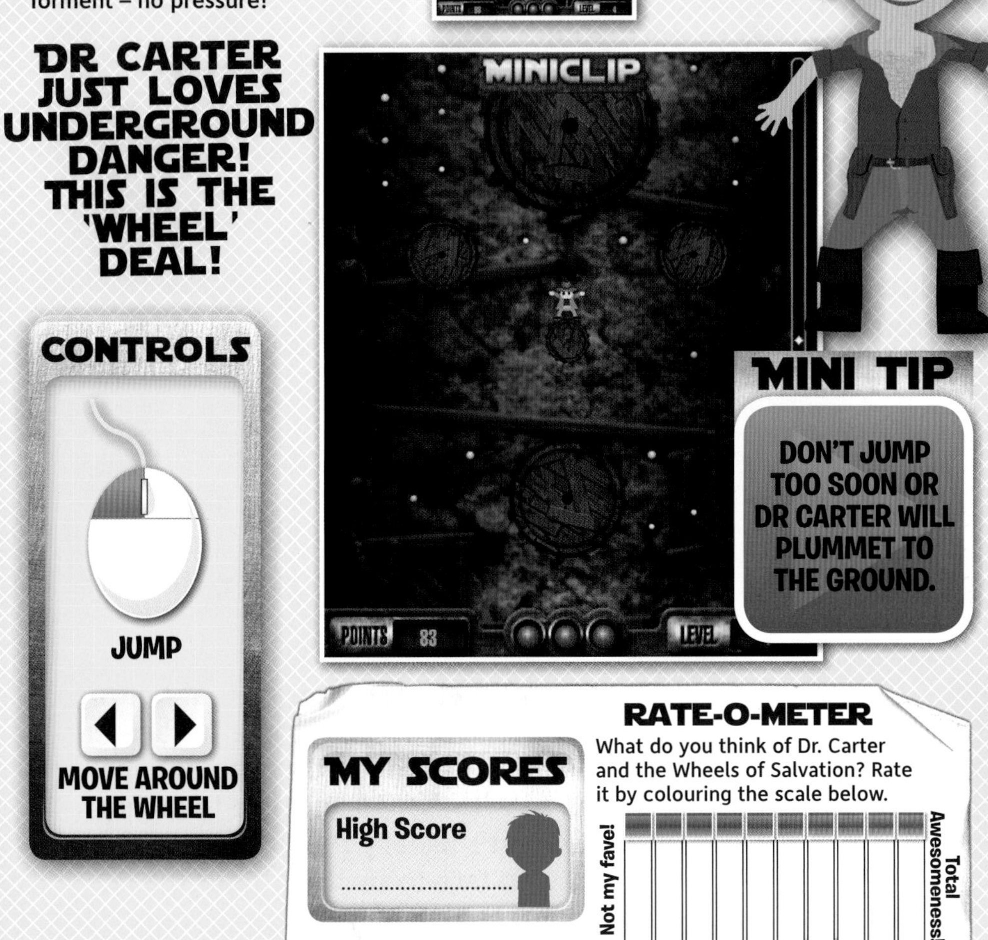

MINI TIP

DON'T JUMP TOO SOON OR DR CARTER WILL PLUMMET TO THE GROUND.

CONTROLS

JUMP

MOVE AROUND THE WHEEL

RATE-O-METER

What do you think of Dr. Carter and the Wheels of Salvation? Rate it by colouring the scale below.

Not my fave! — Total Awesomeness!

MY SCORES

High Score

....

GAME DEVELOPMENT

IT'S NOT JUST A JOB!

You might love sitting around playing games, but do you realise that there are people out there who actually do that for their job? There's no better way to earn your cash than to create an awesome game and then sit back and watch millions of other gamers enjoying it. So, let's take a look at who does what to get a game from idea to screen.

THE PROGRAMMER

The programmers are the pins that holds everything together. They have to take the idea that was in someone's head and make it come to life. If anyone in the team has a problem, it's usually the programmers who stay up late to fix it. Without the programmers, the game just wouldn't exist!

THE PRODUCER

The producer is in charge of the entire game development process from start to finish. They might pull the team together, pay the salaries and keep the whole ship running smoothly. The producer usually has less hands-on game development experience than the rest of the team, but is a good leader.

JOE DESTRUCTO SAMPLE PAGE

SUPERBIKE RACE OFF BEING PROTOTYPED

The Artist

Artists are essential for getting the visual style of any characters, creatures and whole worlds into the game.

The Musician

Music has the potential to make or break a game. A good game can be made great with a fantastic score or soundtrack, like on Extreme Skater (see page 88).

DEVELOP YOUR OWN GAME

To develop your own games, you'll need dedication, skills, tools and ideas. Be patient and take it one step at a time. All our developers started small and simple, then worked their way up. Once you master the basics, you'll be amazed at the results you can get!

STEP 1

COME UP WITH IDEAS

Think about how games work and what makes you keep playing them. Keep a notebook of ideas and, if you want to make any of them into games, team up with friends who have awesome skills in computer programming, art, audio or animation.

STEP 2

FIND THE FUN

Try out a simple version of your game idea as soon as you can. This could be on paper or a quick prototype. If you've got a concept that makes you want to play again, then you're onto a winner!

STEP 3

CREATE PICS, SOUND AND CODE

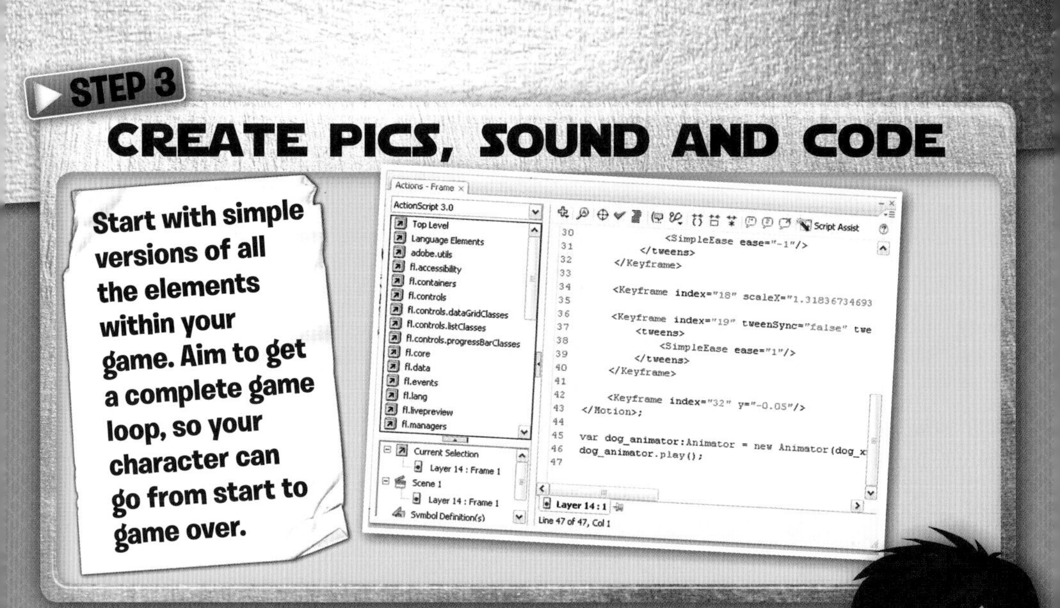

Start with simple versions of all the elements within your game. Aim to get a complete game loop, so your character can go from start to game over.

JONATHAN SAYS ...

The hardest thing about game development is coming up with fresh ideas. Oh, and trying not to play games when you should be working!

JAN SAYS ...

There are lots of free tools and tips on the internet. Search for 'game development tools' and find the best one that suits your needs.

STEP 4

TEST AND POLISH

Once you have the basic game, you can build it up with more levels and better animation. However far you go into your game development career, make sure you have fun and your players will too!

ANDREAS

PAGE 30

FAVE SPORTS GAME:
FREE RUNNING

WHY? This game gives you a real rush! The city scapes are fantastic and put you right in the middle of it all.

HIGH SCORE
50,355

BEN

PAGE 33

FAVE SPORTS GAME:
CHINA 2008

WHY? The amount of different sports that you can take part in is mind-blowing ... and they're all awesome!

HIGH SCORE
17,750

RUTH

PAGE 31

FAVE SPORTS GAME:
MONKEY KICK OFF

WHY? I just love how silly this game is! I mean, come on, it's a monkey kicking a giant coconut!

HIGH SCORE
1,837

ROB L.

PAGE 36

FAVE SPORTS GAME:
EUROPEAN SOCCER CHAMPIONS

WHY? If you can't find me kicking a football about I'll be on this game. Great for footy fans!

HIGH SCORE
4,500

Whether your game is footy, cricket, basketball, white-water rafting or pool, this is the ultimate sports arena. No need for stretching or limbering up here though, just put your mind in the game and set your sights on one thing ... winning!

CHECK OUT A STACK OF CRAZY SPORTS GAMES

WHAT'S IT ABOUT?

This 3D game takes going for a run to a whole new level. Take a fast sprint through a sprawling city, overcoming every obstacle in your way. Jump, climb, grab and roll in this totally funky free-running game. Pull on those trainers and get going ... the city awaits!

MINI TIP

JUMP THROUGH THE MINICLIP STARS TO GAIN 200 POINTS.

RATE-O-METER

What do you think of Free Running? Rate it by colouring the scale below.

Total Awesomeness!

Not my fave!

THROW ON THAT HOODIE, PULL ON THOSE TRAINERS AND GET RUNNING!

ANDREAS' TIP!

YOU'RE AGAINST THE CLOCK, SO FOCUS AND KEEP YOUR EYE ON THE PRIZE.

CONTROLS

Key	Action
▲ ◀ ▼ ▶	RUN
X	JUMP/CLIMB LEDGE

MONKEY KICK OFF™

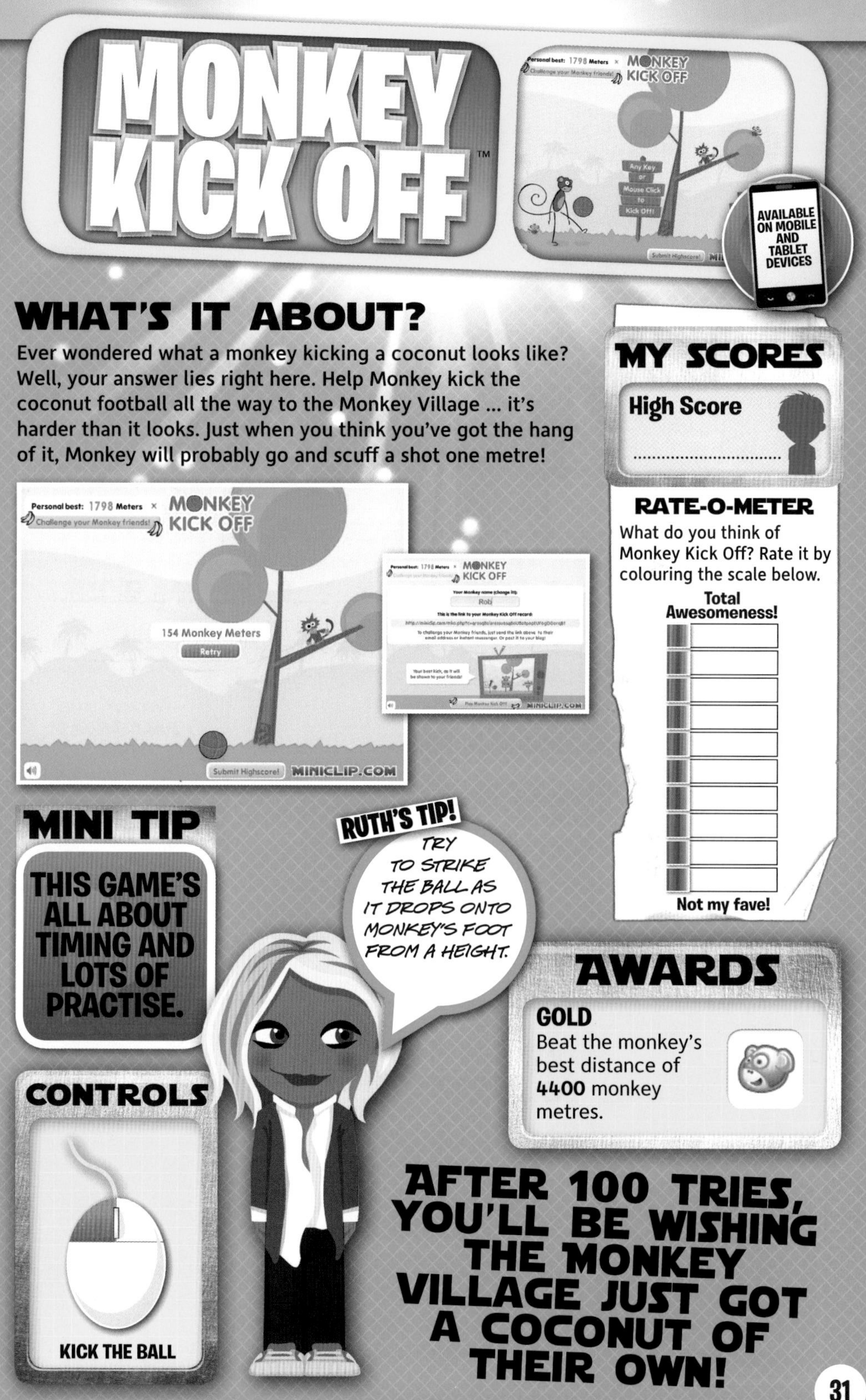

WHAT'S IT ABOUT?

Ever wondered what a monkey kicking a coconut looks like? Well, your answer lies right here. Help Monkey kick the coconut football all the way to the Monkey Village ... it's harder than it looks. Just when you think you've got the hang of it, Monkey will probably go and scuff a shot one metre!

MY SCORES

High Score ....

RATE-O-METER

What do you think of Monkey Kick Off? Rate it by colouring the scale below.

Total Awesomeness!

Not my fave!

MINI TIP

THIS GAME'S ALL ABOUT TIMING AND LOTS OF PRACTISE.

RUTH'S TIP!

TRY TO STRIKE THE BALL AS IT DROPS ONTO MONKEY'S FOOT FROM A HEIGHT.

AWARDS

GOLD
Beat the monkey's best distance of **4400** monkey metres.

CONTROLS

KICK THE BALL

AFTER 100 TRIES, YOU'LL BE WISHING THE MONKEY VILLAGE JUST GOT A COCONUT OF THEIR OWN!

MINICLIP.COM
CRICKET
Defend the Wicket!
Play
CRICKET
DEFEND THE
WICKET
0 Runs
Strike Rate: 0
Best: 1
Instructions: Use the mouse to control the bat.
Game over when the ball hits the stumps or the yellow-and-black zones.
6 Runs
Strike Rate: 1.5
Best: 3
Instructions: Use the mouse to control the bat.
Game over when the ball hits the stumps or the yellow-and-black zones.
WHAT'S IT ABOUT?
It's time to swing your cricket bat and get some points. Try to defend the wicket from the balls and hit as many runs as you can. Stand tall, take a deep breath and prepare to strike. Aim to the right and beat the bowler every time.
ROB'S TIP!
BE CAREFUL NOT TO DOUBLE SWING AND KNOCK THE BALL BEHIND YOU.
CONTROLS
HIT
HOWZAT!
YOU ARE OUT!
7 x 2.33 = 16
Runs S/Rate Score
Try Again
Save High Score
7 Run
20
Instructions: Use the mouse to control the bat.
Game over when the ball hits the stumps or the yellow-and-black zones.
STAND TALL, TAKE A DEEP BREATH AND PREPARE TO STRIKE. HOWZAT!
1
MINI TIP
TRY TO SWING THE BAT AT THE LAST MOMENT FOR MAXIMUM IMPACT.
RATE-O-METER
What do you think of Cricket Defend the Wicket? Rate it by colouring the scale below.
Not my fave!
Total Awesomeness!
MY SCORES
High Score
....

WHAT'S IT ABOUT?

On your marks, get set, go for gold! Aim to get on that podium at the China Games and choose your track and field events to win as many medals as you can. Whether it be 100 metres, long jump, javelin or the hammer throw, you'll need to be a world-class Miniclip athlete to compete!

BEN'S TIP!

FOR JAVELIN AND HAMMER THROWING, WATCH OUT FOR ILLEGAL THROWS.

CONTROLS

Z

SERVE OR SPIKE

X

HOLD DOWN TO RETURN WHILE USING MOUSE TO POSITION RED CIRCLE

MY SCORES

High Score

....

RATE-O-METER

What do you think of China 2008? Rate it by colouring the scale below.

Total Awesomeness!

Not my fave!

MINI TIP

YOU'LL NEED A TRIGGER-HAPPY FINGER ON THAT 'X' BUTTON TO SPRINT WITH THE BEST.

IT'S TIME TO LIMBER UP AND JOINT THE CHINA GAMES ... MINICLIP-STYLE!

URBAN BASKETBALL

WHAT'S IT ABOUT?

Basketball doesn't get more street than this! Take part in some of the toughest street basketball tournaments around and display your insane moves. Put your team together and then block, charge and slam-dunk your way through the competition to prove you're the best in town. Shoot some hoops and take the opposition down!

MY SCORES

High Score

....

RATE-O-METER

What do you think of Urban Basketball? Rate it by colouring the scale below.

Total Awesomeness!

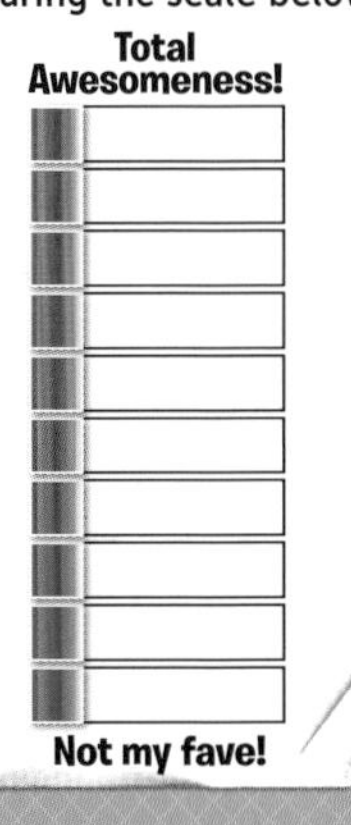

Not my fave!

SLAM-DUNK YOUR WAY THROUGH THE COMPETITION TO PROVE YOU'RE THE BEST!

CONTROLS

MOVE

SHOOT/ TACKLE

BOOST

PASS/ BLOCK

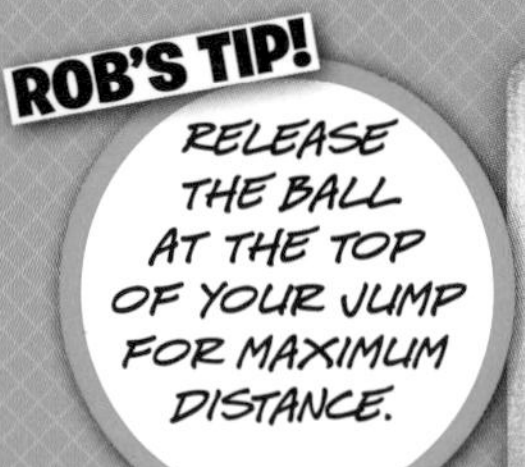

AWARDS

GOLD
Score **100,000 points** in the final showdown.

SILVER
Display your insane skill and score **75,000 points**.

BRONZE
Slam-dunk your way to **50,000 points**.

EXTREME PAMPLONA

WHAT'S IT ABOUT?

Run, run as fast as you can! You'll have to move pretty quickly in this series of action-packed levels that take you though nine countries. There's no time to rest, even from the beginning, as you have to outrun a raging bull, hot on your tail through the streets of Spain. In the UK, you'll have to outrun a truncheon-waving policeman. Get moving and don't look back!

ROB'S TIP!

TRY TO JUMP FROM HIGH OBJECTS. THIS WILL GIVE YOU MORE DISTANCE.

RUN, RUN AS FAST AS YOU CAN! DON'T LOOK BACK AND GET MOVING!

RATE-O-METER

What do you think of Extreme Pamplona? Rate it by colouring the scale below.

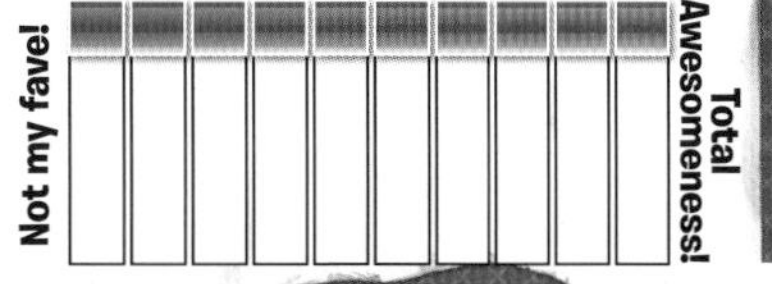

EUROPEAN SOCCER CHAMPIONS

WHAT'S IT ABOUT?

You've travelled to the European Soccer Championship and the nation's hopes rest on your shoulders. You've assembled your squad of world-class players and now it's time to do your talking on the pitch. It will be the toughest and fastest 90 minutes of your life, but keep your eye on the prize and aim to lift the trophy!

HIT THE BACK OF THE NET AND MAKE THE CROWD ROAR!

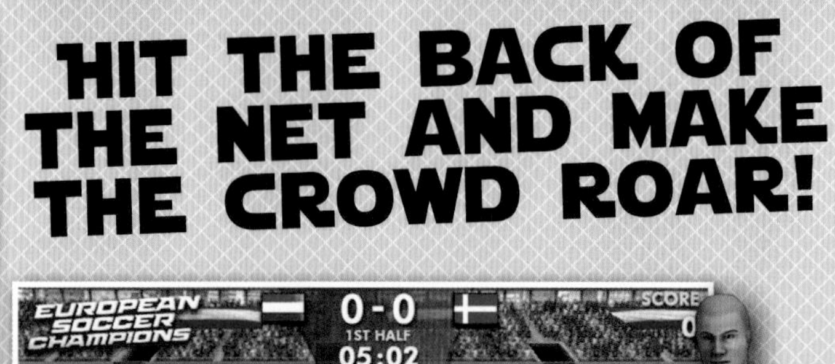

AWARDS

Gold
Win the Championship and score at least **155,000 points.**

Silver
Play well at the Championship and score at least **75,000 points.**

Bronze
Although you play well, you are unlucky and only score **35,000 points.**

IT'S THE TOUGHEST AND FASTEST 90 MINUTES OF YOUR LIFE!

MINI TIP

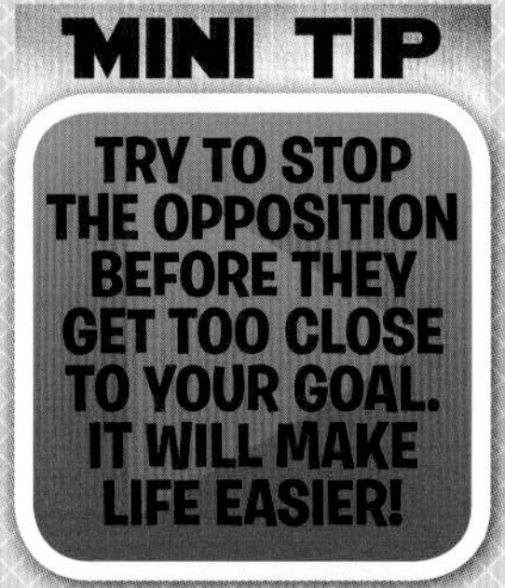

TRY TO STOP THE OPPOSITION BEFORE THEY GET TOO CLOSE TO YOUR GOAL. IT WILL MAKE LIFE EASIER!

MY SCORES

High Score

....

RATE-O-METER

What do you think of European Soccer Champions? Rate it by colouring the scale below.

Total Awesomeness!

Not my fave!

ROB L.'S TIP!

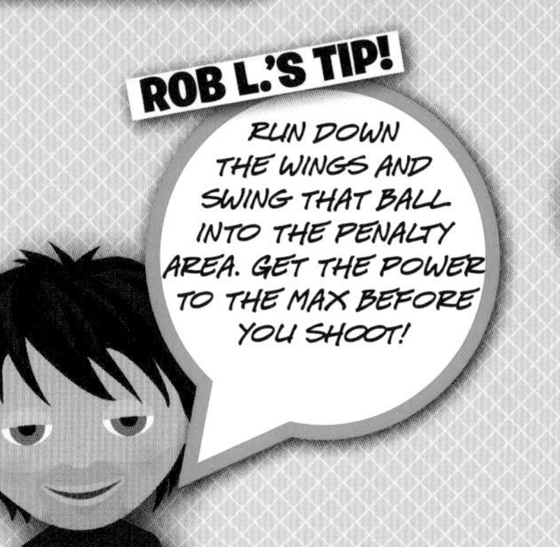

MOUNTAIN BIKE

WHAT'S IT ABOUT?

Race against the clock in a series of exciting mountain bike challenges. Speed across rough terrain, leaning into the hills and keeping perfect balance at all times. Hit those pedals, let the wheels turn and get racing. But keep your mind on some tricks, too. This game ain't all about the speed ... it's about how you handle your wheels!

CONTROLS

◀ ▶ TILT THE BIKE LEFT AND RIGHT

▲ ▼ ACCELERATE AND BRAKE

SPACE CHANGE DIRECTION

THIS GAME AIN'T ALL ABOUT THE SPEED ... IT'S ABOUT HOW YOU HANDLE YOUR WHEELS!

MINI TIP

LEAN FORWARD AS YOU GO UP HILLS TO INCREASE YOUR SPEED.

MY SCORES

High Score ....

RATE-O-METER

What do you think of Mountain Bike? Rate it by colouring the scale below.

Not my fave! — Total Awesomeness!

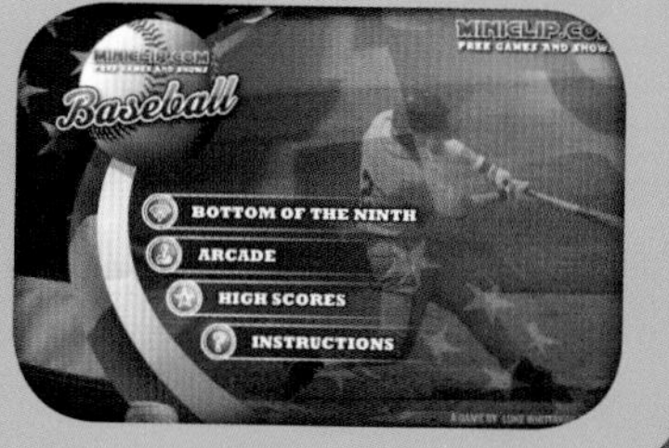

WHAT'S IT ABOUT?

It is bottom of the ninth and you're two runs down. This is as tense as it gets. Can you rally your team to win the game with only 2 outs left? It'll be tough, but it's time to step up to the plate. There's also an arcade version of the game if you want to mix things up. Grab that bat and get in the swing!

GRAB THAT BAT, STEP UP TO THE PLATE AND GET IN THE SWING!

CONTROLS

AIM

BAT

MINI TIP

TRY NOT TO HIT STRAIGHT TOWARDS AN OUTFIELD PLAYER. IF THEY CATCH IT, YOU'RE OUT!

MY SCORES

High Score ....

RATE-O-METER

What do you think of Baseball? Rate it by colouring the scale below.

Total Awesomeness!

Not my fave!

ROB'S TIP!

SLICE OR HOOK THE BALL AS YOU HIT IT. THAT WILL MAKE LIFE HARDER FOR THE OPPOSITION.

YoMe CELEBRITY STYLES

Ever wondered what some celebrity YoMe's might look like? Well, here they are! We had great fun creating these celeb looks. There's loads more online, but here's a select few to give you a taster!

ANGELINA JOLIE

MOVIES ...

JACK SPARROW

TOM CRUISE

LINDSAY LOHAN

BRAD PITT

INDIANA JONES

Clear the red carpet and make way for YoMe movie madess with this group of A-List stars!

MUSIC ...
These singing and dancing music legends are some of the hottest stars on the planet. Now we have them as YoMe's, we just need some YoMusic to go with them!
SNOOP DOG
EMINEM
BEYONCÉ
SHAKIRA
P DIDDY
BONO
JUSTIN TIMBERLAKE
LUDACRIS

JAMIE

PAGE 45

FAVE 3D GAME:
SALOON BRAWL

WHY? The Wild West was a mean place. This crazy game gives you the chance to be the ultimate outlaw.

HIGH SCORE
57,826

KIERAN

PAGE 44

FAVE 3D GAME:
RHINO RUSH

WHY? This is a fun mission that allows you to go through obstacles as a rhino in pants and ultimately save the day!

ROB

PAGE 46

FAVE 3D GAME:
GAS & SAND

WHY? This is the most face-meltingly fast game around! The slick cars and rad scenes are cool too.

RUTH

PAGE 53

FAVE 3D GAME:
BOWMASTER

WHY? Soooo addictive! After just one go, you want to be the best archer in the land.

3D GAMES

These games have got awesome visuals that rival the insane game play. It's like you're actually in the gaming world, so if you're scared of quad biking, flying upside-down or being jabbed by a streetwise boxer, then maybe this 3D area isn't for you!

CHECK OUT A STACK OF ULTRA COOL 3D GAMES

RHINO RUSH

WHAT'S IT ABOUT?

You are a little blue rhino with a giant horn and pants on! You're all alone in the world. Why? Because all your friends have been captured by the Evil Baboon. Well, don't just stand there ... go from zero to hero and rescue your kidnapped herd. Stampede forward, jump over obstacles, defeat the baboons and save the day. Chaaaarge!

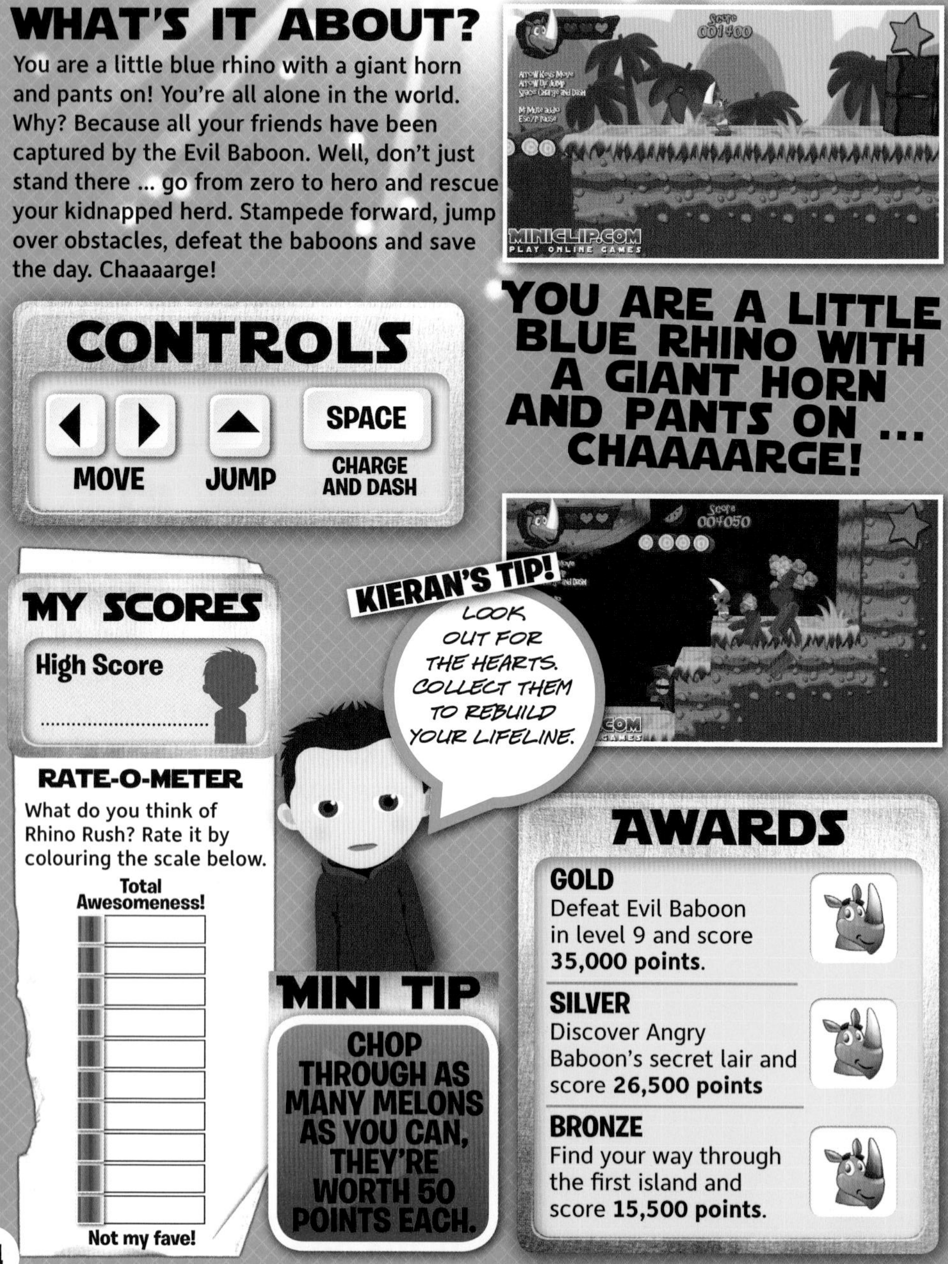

YOU ARE A LITTLE BLUE RHINO WITH A GIANT HORN AND PANTS ON ... CHAAAAARGE!

CONTROLS

◀ ▶	▲	SPACE
MOVE	JUMP	CHARGE AND DASH

MY SCORES

High Score ....

RATE-O-METER

What do you think of Rhino Rush? Rate it by colouring the scale below.

Total Awesomeness!

Not my fave!

MINI TIP

CHOP THROUGH AS MANY MELONS AS YOU CAN, THEY'RE WORTH 50 POINTS EACH.

AWARDS

GOLD
Defeat Evil Baboon in level 9 and score **35,000 points**.

SILVER
Discover Angry Baboon's secret lair and score **26,500 points**

BRONZE
Find your way through the first island and score **15,500 points**.

SALOON BRAWL

WHAT'S IT ABOUT?

Yeehaw, partners! It's time to saddle up and head west. But the town you're heading to ain't no holiday camp. This is one of the meanest and roughest places around. You're thrown into a saloon smack bang in the middle of a brawl. There's no time to stop and think in here or you're dead meat.

MINI TIP

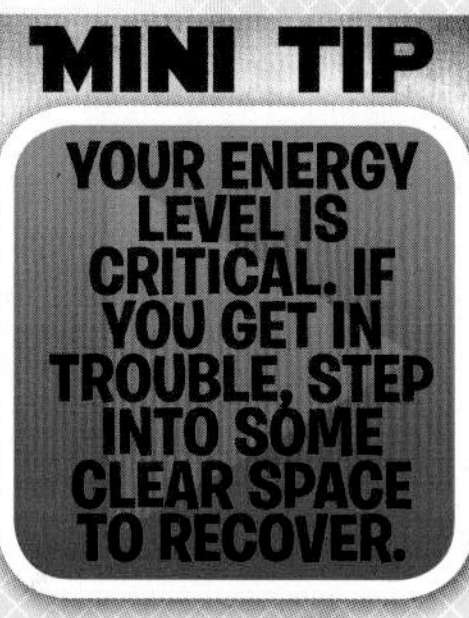

GRAB YOUR FOES, THROW OBJECTS AND BECOME THE ULTIMATE OUTLAW. YEEHAW!

JAMIE'S TIP!

GRAB ANY FIRST AID BOTTLES YOU SEE, THEY'LL RESTORE YOUR ENERGY. DON'T GET KO'D!

CONTROLS

- Arrow keys: MOVE
- Z: BLOCK
- X: PUNCH
- C: GRAB
- SPACE: SPECIAL ATTACK

AWARDS

GOLD
Take down the biggest, meanest cowboy in the saloon and score **60,000 points**.

SILVER
KO every ruffian in the place and score **40,000 points**.

BRONZE
These cowboys mean trouble. Score **20,000 points** by knocking them out.

MY SCORES

High Score ....

RATE-O-METER

What do you think of Saloon Brawl? Rate it by colouring the scale below.

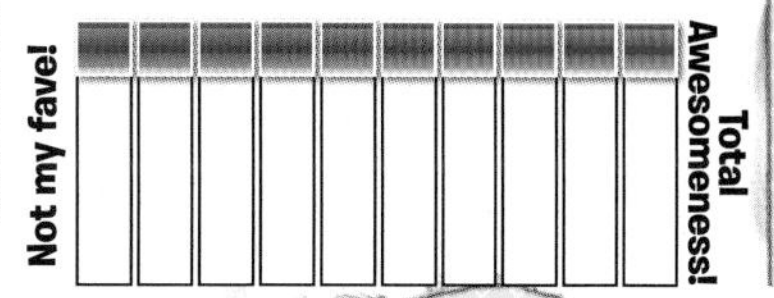

GAS & SAND™

WHAT'S IT ABOUT?

It's one of the fastest, most adrenaline-pumping games around. Jump behind the wheel of a racing car and battle it out for first place around this ancient arena racetrack. Oh, by the way, the race is on sand, so taking those corners is only for pros. If you have a need for speed then what are you waiting for? Grab the wheel and hit the gas!

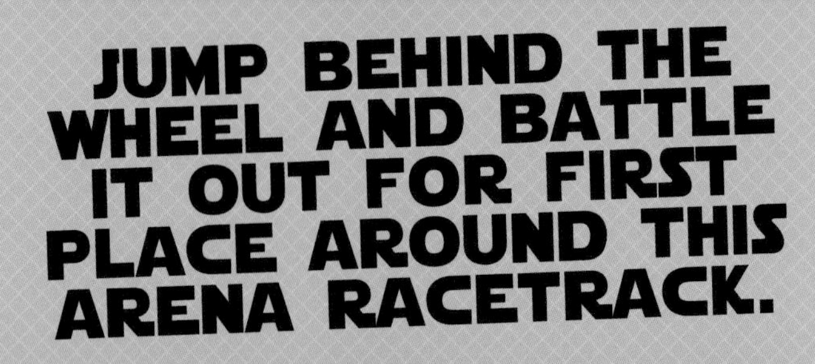

MINI TIP

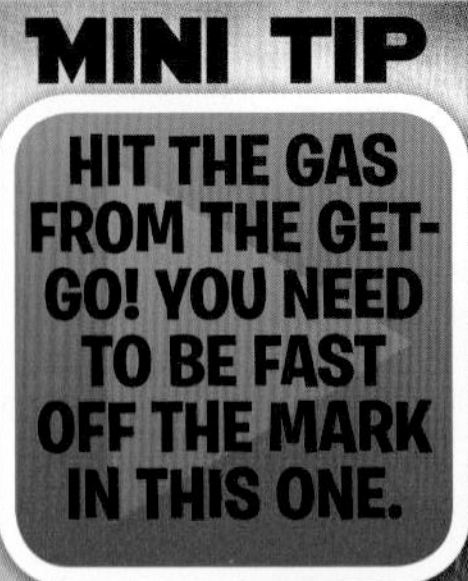

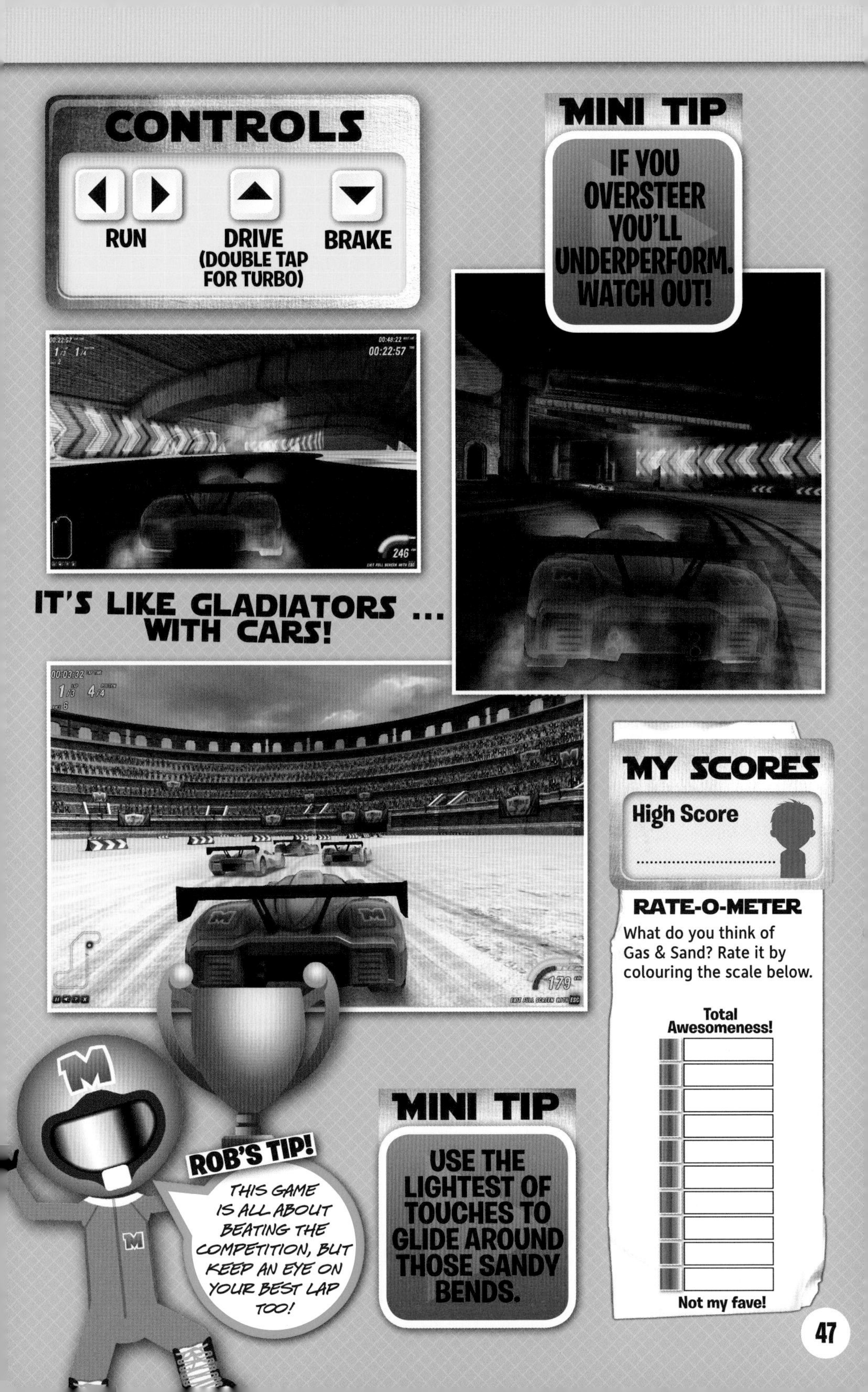
CONTROLS
RUN
DRIVE (DOUBLE TAP FOR TURBO)
BRAKE
MINI TIP
IF YOU OVERSTEER YOU'LL UNDERPERFORM. WATCH OUT!
IT'S LIKE GLADIATORS ... WITH CARS!
MY SCORES
High Score
RATE-O-METER
What do you think of Gas & Sand? Rate it by colouring the scale below.
Total Awesomeness!
Not my fave!
ROB'S TIP!
THIS GAME IS ALL ABOUT BEATING THE COMPETITION, BUT KEEP AN EYE ON YOUR BEST LAP TOO!
MINI TIP
USE THE LIGHTEST OF TOUCHES TO GLIDE AROUND THOSE SANDY BENDS.

ON THE RUN VEGAS™

WHAT'S IT ABOUT?

You're a fugitive on the run from the CIA and there's no better place to give 'em a chase than Las Vegas! You barely outsmarted the undercover cops as you boarded the plane to the entertainment capital of the world, and now it's time to hit The Strip and rip up the tarmac. The police have you in their sights, so only the fastest fugitive will win big in this town!

ROB'S TIP!

FOR ULTIMATE HAIRPIN BENDS, HIT THE HANDBRAKE AND LOSE THE COPS.

THERE'S NO BETTER PLACE TO GIVE 'EM A CHASE THAN VEGAS!

AWARDS

GOLD
Hit the jackpot and get your total up to **25,000 points** to win the ultimate award.

SILVER
Know Vegas like the back of your hand and score **20,000 points**.

BRONZE
Rip up the streets, burn some rubber and score **10,00 points**.

GAMES IN THE SERIES

ON THE RUN
All chases have to start somewhere, and On the Run is where it all goes down. The CIA will stop at nothing to catch you. The chase is on!

ON THE RUN 2
You hold highly classified information and the CIA are out to recover it. You must get on the move, and fast. Drive to the airport and get on that plane ... no matter the cost!

ONLY THE FASTEST FUGITIVE WINS BIG IN THIS TOWN!

MY SCORES

High Score

....

RATE-O-METER
What do you think of On The Run Vegas? Rate it by colouring the scale below.

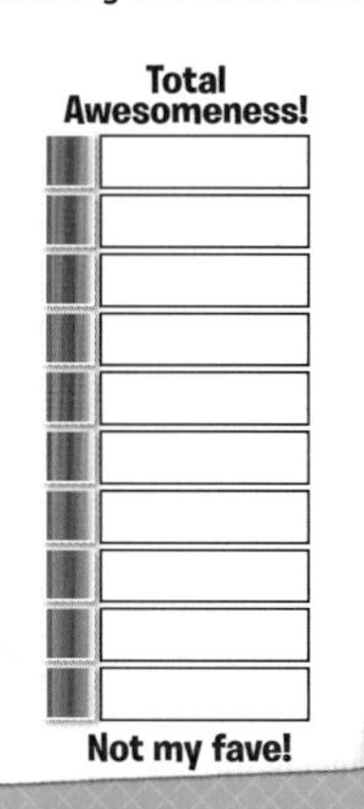

AGE OF SPEED 2

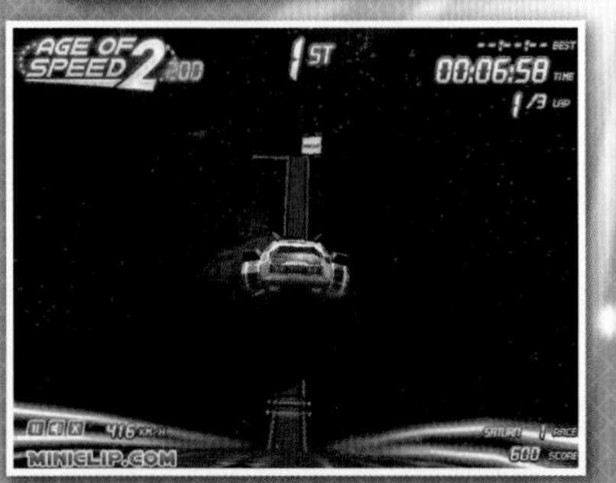

WHAT'S IT ABOUT?

This racing game is literally out of this world. Hop into the most futuristic car around and head to the best circuits in the universe. This neon race track is more like a roller coaster than a Grand Prix circuit as you must master loop the loops, colossal jumps and corkscrews to win. Choose your car, rev it up and blast off!

CONTROLS

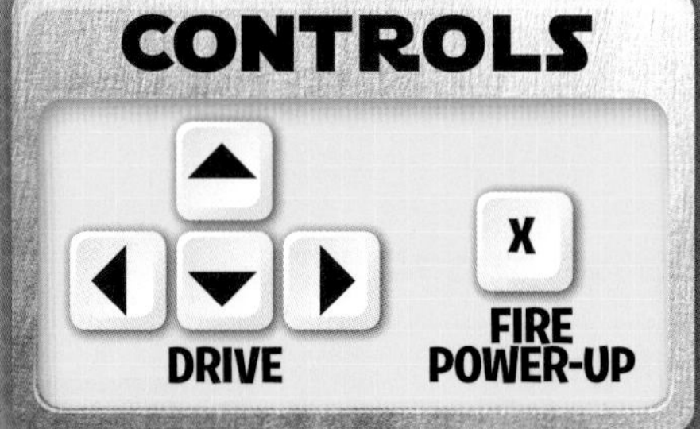

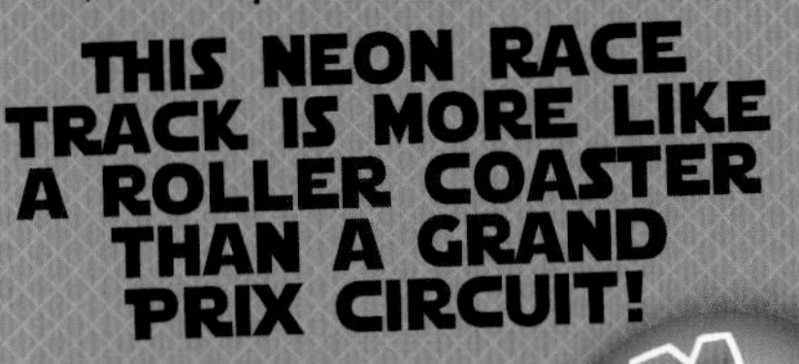

ROB'S TIP!

WHEN YOU'RE LEADING, LOOK OUT FOR THE SPACE-AGE SHIELD. THIS WILL PROTECT YOUR CAR.

AGE OF SPEED

It's not set in space, but these tracks are definitely in another world. Pick your car and head to the first track – it's in the clouds, so you'll need a head for heights to compete!

MY SCORES

High Score

....

RATE-O-METER

What do you think of Age of Speed 2? Rate it by colouring the scale below.

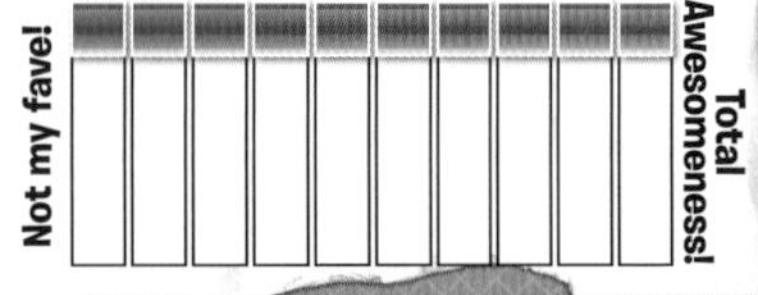

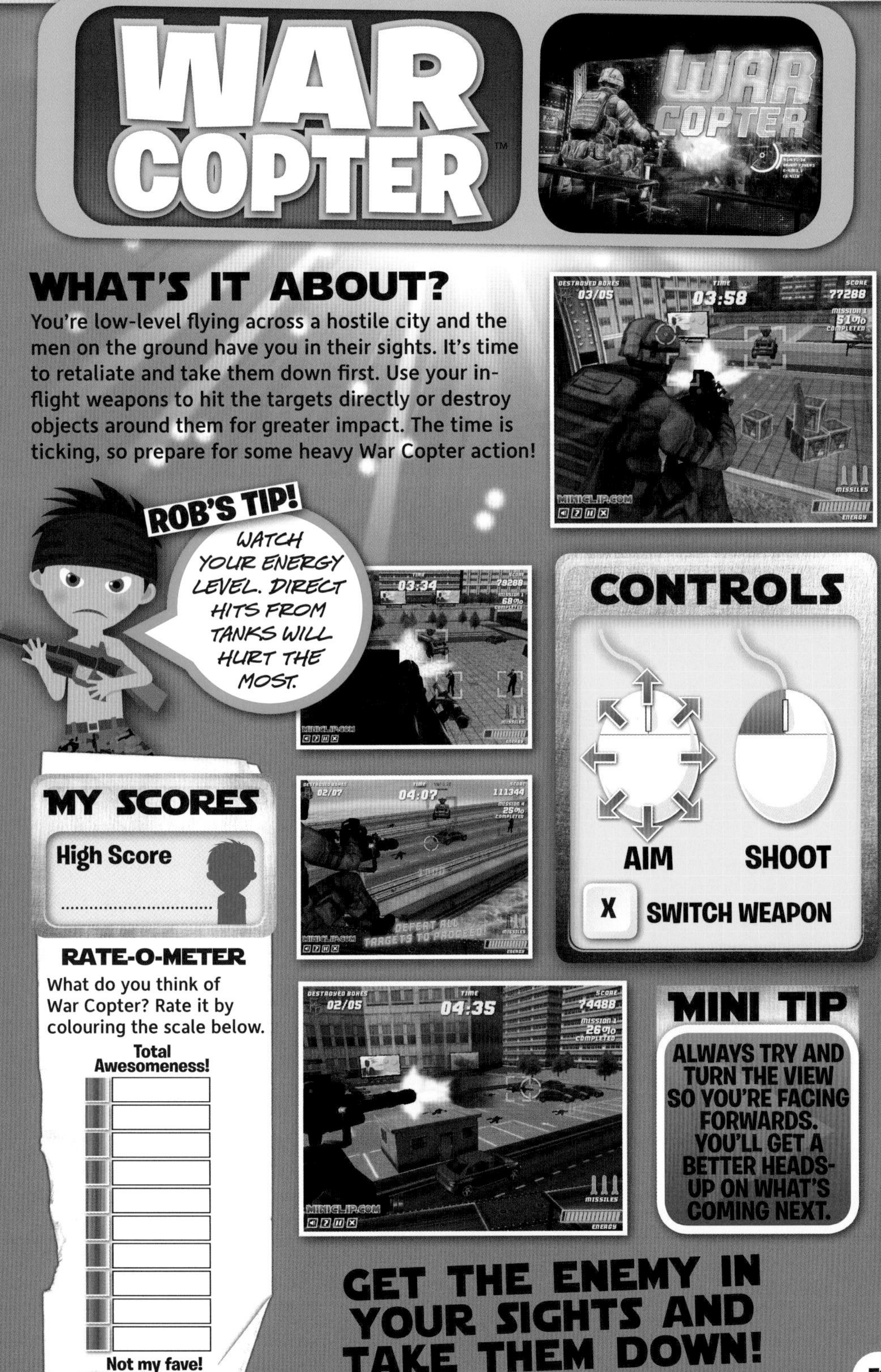
WAR COPTER™
WHAT'S IT ABOUT?
You're low-level flying across a hostile city and the men on the ground have you in their sights. It's time to retaliate and take them down first. Use your in-flight weapons to hit the targets directly or destroy objects around them for greater impact. The time is ticking, so prepare for some heavy War Copter action!
ROB'S TIP!
WATCH YOUR ENERGY LEVEL. DIRECT HITS FROM TANKS WILL HURT THE MOST.
CONTROLS
AIM
SHOOT
X
SWITCH WEAPON
MY SCORES
High Score
RATE-O-METER
What do you think of War Copter? Rate it by colouring the scale below.
Total Awesomeness!
Not my fave!
MINI TIP
ALWAYS TRY AND TURN THE VIEW SO YOU'RE FACING FORWARDS. YOU'LL GET A BETTER HEADS-UP ON WHAT'S COMING NEXT.
GET THE ENEMY IN YOUR SIGHTS AND TAKE THEM DOWN!

DOGFIGHT

WHAT'S IT ABOUT?

It's time to take to the skies and battle your enemies in this dog-eat-dog aerial combat game. Before you risk your life, make sure you get in some training where you can practice flying and shooting targets. Once you're ready, then prepare for lift-off and let battle commence!

MY SCORES

High Score ....

RATE-O-METER

What do you think of Dogfight? Rate it by colouring the scale below.

Total Awesomeness!

Not my fave!

CONTROLS

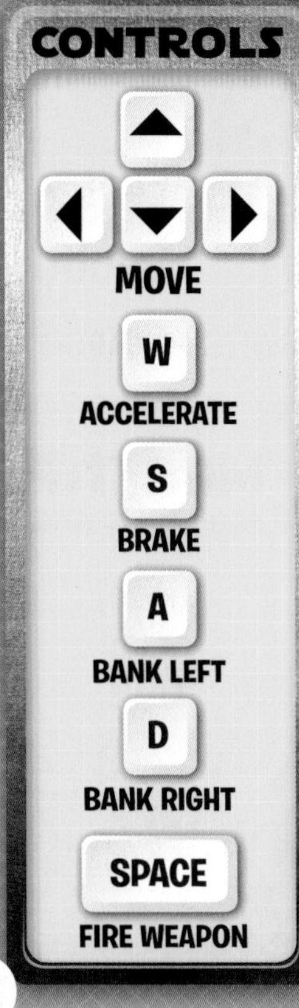

MOVE

W ACCELERATE

S BRAKE

A BANK LEFT

D BANK RIGHT

SPACE FIRE WEAPON

IT'S YOUR TIME, ACE! TAKE THE CONTROLS AND LET THE DOGFIGHT BEGIN!

MINI TIP

ONCE YOU GET IN THE SKY YOU'RE FIGHTING OTHER ONLINE PLAYERS, SO WATCH OUT!

ROB'S TIP!

REMEMBER TO HEAD TO THE HANGER WHERE YOU CAN UPGRADE YOUR MACHINERY.

BOW MASTER™

WHAT'S IT ABOUT?

Master the art of archery and change your fate in this game. Not only do you need to have the aim of a champion, but the clock is against you, too. Score as many points as you can within the time as you take on these medieval challenges. Arrows at the ready, archers – it's target time!

MINI TIP

THE BLUE STRIP ON THE BOW IS THE LEVEL YOUR ARROW WILL HIT ITS TARGET.

CONTROLS

HOLD, DRAW AND RELEASE TO FIRE.

RUTH'S TIP!

THE MOVING TARGETS ARE PRETTY HARD TO HIT. WATCH THEM FOR A WHILE FIRST TO WORK OUT WHEN TO SHOOT. DON'T RUN OUT OF TIME, THOUGH!

GAMES IN THE SERIES

WINTER BOW MASTER

Add some snow to your bow in this original festive version of the game.

MY SCORES

High Score

....

RATE-O-METER

What do you think of Bow Master? Rate it by colouring the scale below.

Not my fave! — Total Awesomeness!

AWARDS

Take a look at this selection of amazing awards that you can win just by playing Miniclip games! Why not go through and put a tick next to the ones you've been awesome enough to win?

IN-GAME AWARDS

MIMELET
APACHE OVERKILL
CANARY GOLD
8 BALL POOL MULTIPLAYER TOURNAMENT FINALIST
2
AMERICAN FOOTBALL GREEN
GIFT KEEPER CHRISTMAS
GARDEN GNOME CARNAGE AWARD
WORLD CRICKET 2011 WORLD CHALLENGE WINNER
YOUDA FARMER 2 GOLD
X3
ROBO RAMPAGE TRIPLE KILL
TURKEY RUN
ALL GOLD
ZOIKZ 2 GOLD
CANDY MAGIC GOLD
FUNNY QUOTES
YOUDA SURVIVOR GOLD
EPIC COASTER EPIC SURVIVAL
FRAGGER LOST CITY AWARD
FLING GOLD ARCADE
WORM FOOD GOLD
SOCCER STARS GOLD
GALAXY GUNNER GOLD
TROY GOLD
DINO STRIKE FOSSIL FUELED
BULLETHEAD GOLD
PIRATE GOLF GOLD
10
ANAGRAM MAGIC 10 STREAK
R.I.F.T. GOLD
1
WINTER GAMES GOLD
PEST CONTROL GOLD
MOVIE MUNCHIES GOLD
CLICKPLAY GOLD
ICY SLICY GOLD
SNOW TALE GOLD
COMMANDO DT COMPLETE
UP BEAT BLUE UP BEAT
CLASSROOM PILOT GOLD-PLATED PAPER PLANE
DUNE BUGGY
A
ALPHATTACK COMMANDER
GEMAICA GOLD
SCOOBY DOO GOLD
MORE AWESOME
AWARDS
OVER THE PAGE!

AWARDS
AGENT FREERIDE 2 GOLD
OUTPOST SWARM LOCK PICKER
ZOMBIE DOLLS SILVER
WONDERPUTT GOLD
WORD COLLAPSE FAMOUS QUOTES
GEMAICA SILVER AWARD
AWESOME TANKS ULTRACOMBO
RUBBLE TROUBLE MOSCOW GOLD
LAVALAB GOLD
CACTUS McCOY 2 GOLD
BULLFROG POKER COSA FROGSTA
GO SANTA GO GOLD
COMMANDO III MASTER
EXTREME QUAD GOLD
GHOSTFIRE ATTACK GOLD
BAJA MOTOCROSS GOLD
SUPERCYCLONE GOLD
AREA ZERO HARD MODE
ASTEROID RUSH GOLD
TOYS VS NIGHTMARES SKELETON
K-MILLION GOLD
JOE DESTRUCTION LEAD LUNCH
ALL ON MAX!
ROBO RAMPAGE TO THE MAX
STUNT CRAZY GOLDEN
MONSTER ISLAND SPARE
ASSAULT COURSE GOLD
SUPER ROBOT WAR GOLD
RETROSHOOT 360 GOLD
URBAN BASKETBALL GOLD
NOTEPAD CHAOS AWASRD
CANYON DEFENSE 2 LEIUTENANT
RED CODE 3 GOLD
RIVER RAIDER GOLD
SHORT HISTORY OF THE WORLD BOY WONDER
DECAJUMP LEAD BALLOON
ARCTIC DRIFT GOLD
ON THE RUN 2 GOLD
DECAJUMP TIME TRAVELER
LIGHT TEMPLE GOLD
WORLD CRICKET 2011 TAIL END BATSMAN
ROBO RAMPAGE CLOSE CALL
FREE RUNNING GOLD

ADDITIONAL AWARDS

ANDREAS

PAGE 60

FAVE MULTIPLAYER GAME:
RUNESCAPE

WHY? A great role-play game that takes you on a mad medieval quest with monsters, dragons and trolls.

KIERAN

PAGE 67

FAVE MULTIPLAYER GAME:
BOXO

WHY? Awesome Mayan multiplayer where you can challenge your friends to find out who's ruler of the gems.

SYLVIA

PAGE 63

FAVE MULTIPLAYER GAME:
5 IN A ROW

WHY? A classic game, we all know the rules, but now I can play with pals from around the world.

TITO

PAGE 64

FAVE MULTIPLAYER GAME:
8 BALL POOL MULTIPLAYER

WHY? I love the fact that I can play in international pool tournaments from the comfort of home!

HIGH SCORE
WIN % 60.4

MULTIPLAYER GAMES

It's time to move outside your comfort zone and take the challenge to the world. Our multiplayer games allow you to play in real-time against friends and unknown opposition. Here's the place to rack up your scores and see how you stack up against the competition!

CHECK OUT A STACK OF
MAD MULTIPLAYER GAMES

WHAT'S IT ABOUT?

Join the medieval fantasy world of Gielinor to fight, quest or just hang out. This is the most popular free-to-play online role-playing game in the world with tons of skills to master, hundreds of quests to complete and thousands of monsters to slay. The graphics are plain awesome and the game play is advanced, as you decide where you want to go and what you want to do. If you love quests, dragons and trolls then head to Gielinor ... now!

FOR THE QUEST-LOVING, DRAGON-SLAYING, TROLL-FIGHTING GAMER!

ABOUT GIELINOR

Gielinor is a fantasy realm split into many kingdoms and regions. Most of the game is played on foot, but you can also charter ships to sail around. There's always many challenges in each area of the game, but it starts off with a walkthrough tutorial to help you learn the ropes before you embark on your journey.

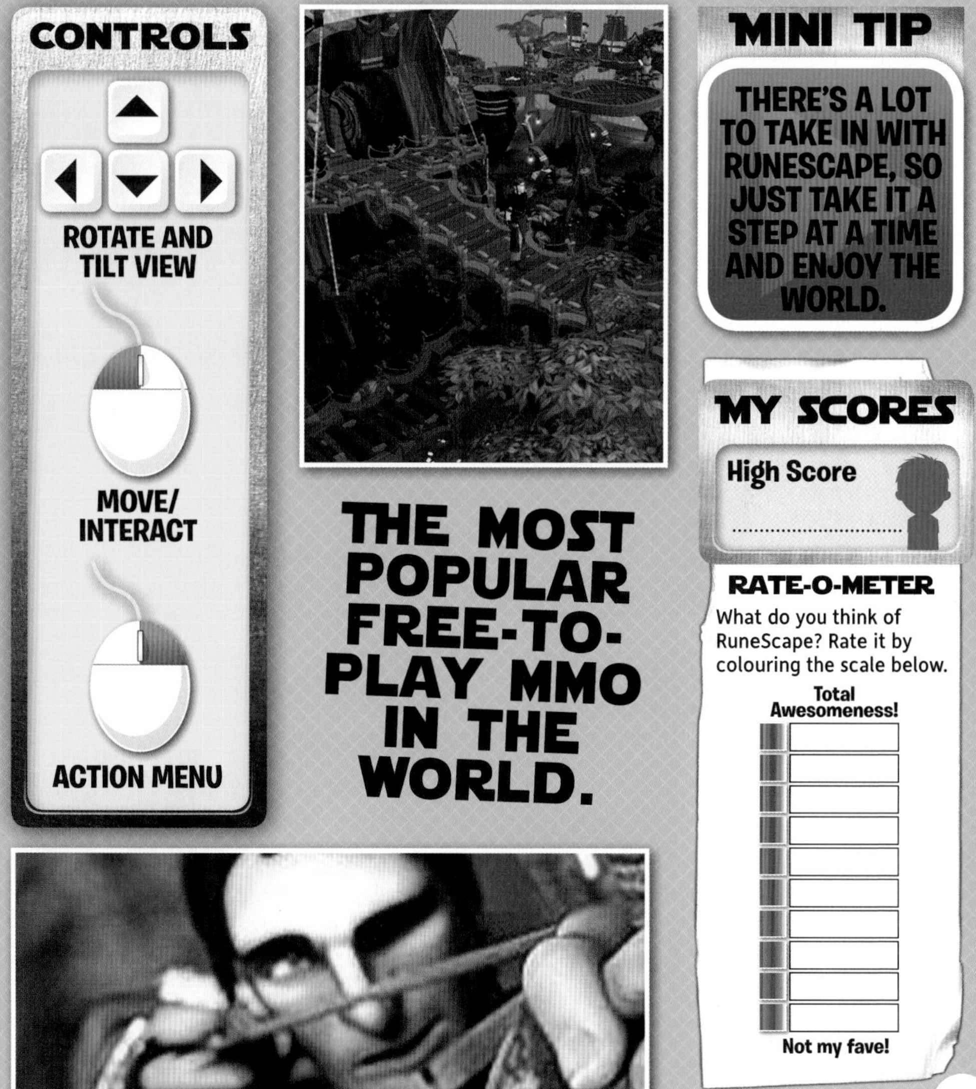

CONTROLS

ROTATE AND TILT VIEW

MOVE/ INTERACT

ACTION MENU

MINI TIP

THERE'S A LOT TO TAKE IN WITH RUNESCAPE, SO JUST TAKE IT A STEP AT A TIME AND ENJOY THE WORLD.

THE MOST POPULAR FREE-TO-PLAY MMO IN THE WORLD.

MY SCORES

High Score

....

RATE-O-METER

What do you think of RuneScape? Rate it by colouring the scale below.

Total Awesomeness!

Not my fave!

MONKEY SNOWFIGHT

WHAT'S IT ABOUT?

The idea is simple ... whack the other monkey with snowballs and 'nana bombs! Play live, online games against real opponents. Load your snowball shooter, aim, get the speed right and fire. But it's not that easy! You'll have to shoot over partition walls and avoid obstacles to win.

GO BANANAS ON YOUR OPPONENT IN THIS WACKY SNOWBALL FIGHT!

MY SCORES

High Score

....

RATE-O-METER

What do you think of Monkey Snowfight? Rate it by colouring the scale below.

Total Awesomeness!

Not my fave!

CONTROLS

TO AIM AND FIRE

ROB'S TIP!

MAKE SURE YOU'RE PRETTY GOOD. IF YOU PLAY A DULL GAME, YOUR OPPONENT MIGHT LEAVE!

MINI TIP

PICK UP BONUSES TO STAY IN THE GAME LONGER.

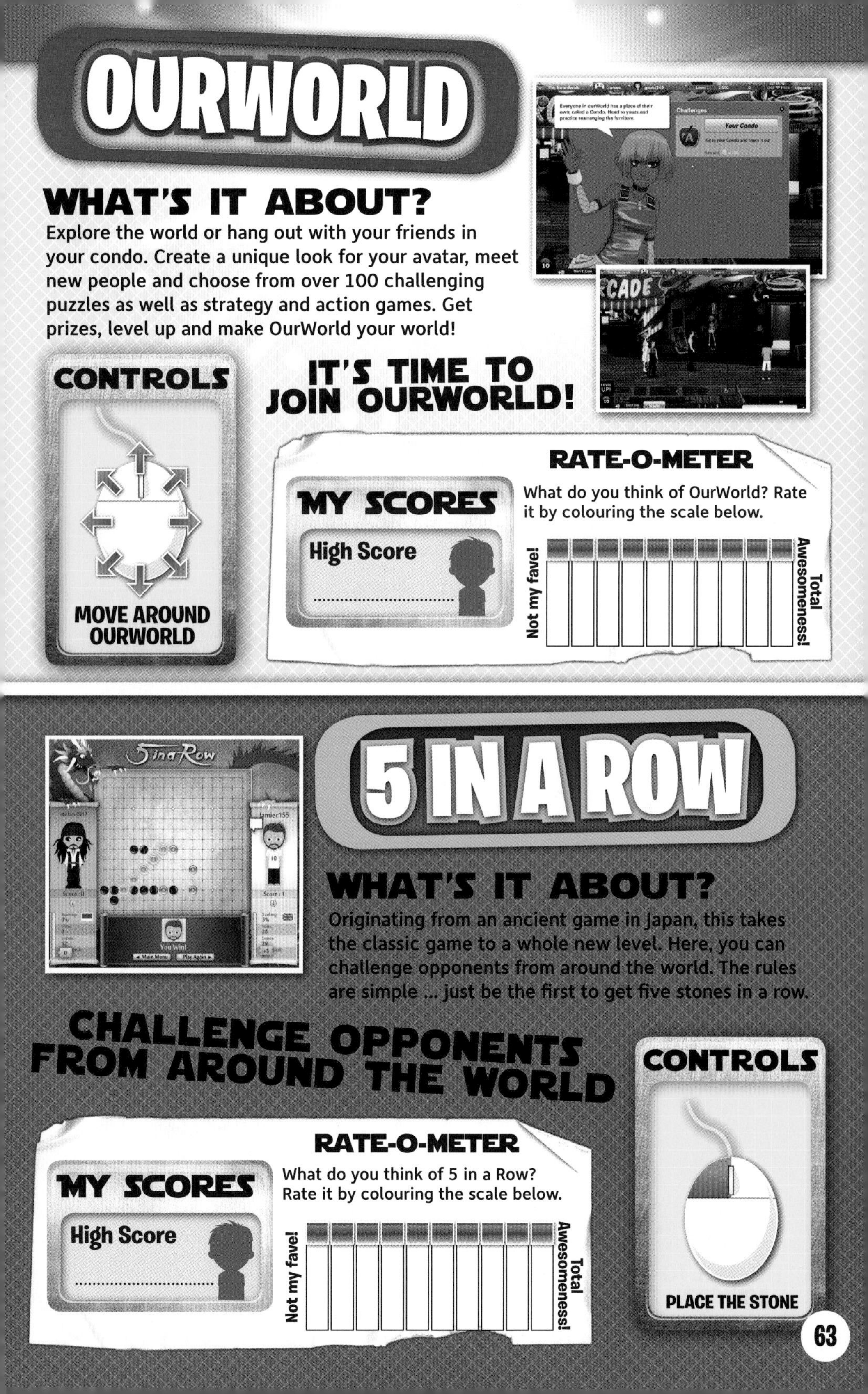

OURWORLD

WHAT'S IT ABOUT?

Explore the world or hang out with your friends in your condo. Create a unique look for your avatar, meet new people and choose from over 100 challenging puzzles as well as strategy and action games. Get prizes, level up and make OurWorld your world!

CONTROLS

MOVE AROUND OURWORLD

IT'S TIME TO JOIN OURWORLD!

MY SCORES

High Score ....

RATE-O-METER

What do you think of OurWorld? Rate it by colouring the scale below.

Not my fave! — Total Awesomeness!

5 IN A ROW

WHAT'S IT ABOUT?

Originating from an ancient game in Japan, this takes the classic game to a whole new level. Here, you can challenge opponents from around the world. The rules are simple ... just be the first to get five stones in a row.

CHALLENGE OPPONENTS FROM AROUND THE WORLD

CONTROLS

PLACE THE STONE

MY SCORES

High Score ....

RATE-O-METER

What do you think of 5 in a Row? Rate it by colouring the scale below.

Not my fave! — Total Awesomeness!

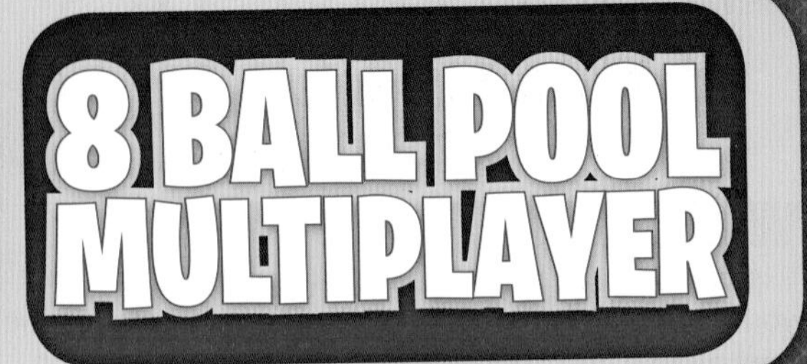

8 BALL POOL MULTIPLAYER

WHAT'S IT ABOUT?

It's time to shoot some pool against live online players. Get all the action of the pool hall without leaving your home. This game is so realistic and addictive you'll never want to give up the challenge.

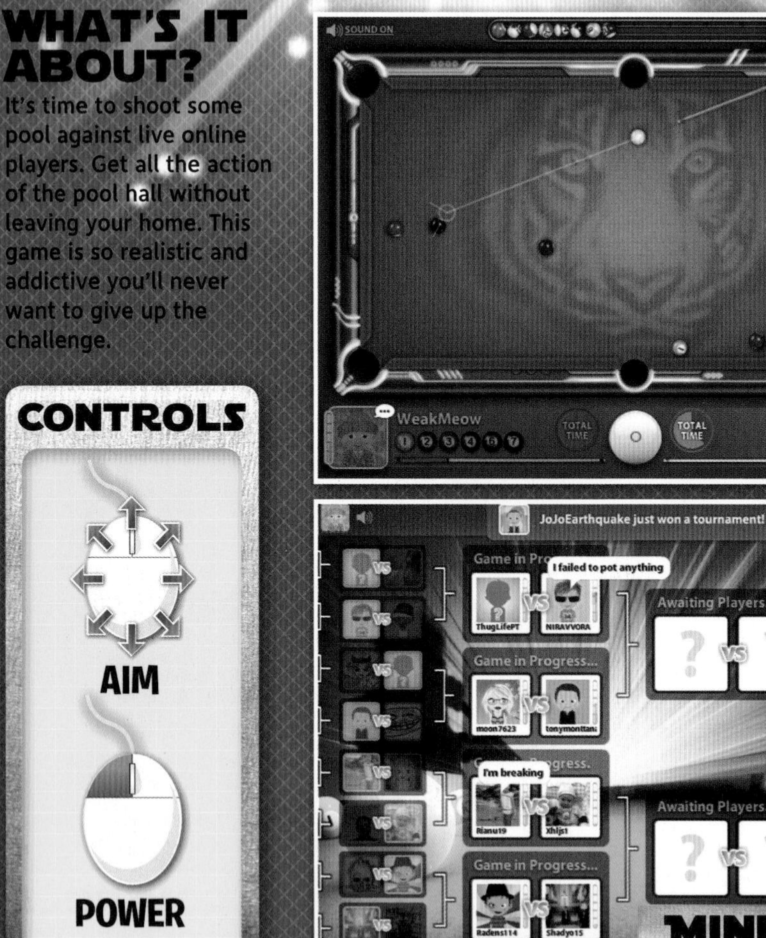

CONTROLS

MINI TIP

YOU CAN VISIT THE SHOP TO BUY AWESOME POOL CUES AND TABLES.

AWARDS

THERE ARE 36 AWARDS TO WIN. HERE'S A FEW OF THEM!

8 Ball Win
Win a game of 8 Ball Pool.

8 Ball Master
Win **1000** games.

Denial
Win without your opponent getting a shot!

Hotter Streak
Win **10** games in a row.

Combo Shot
Pot 3 or more of your object ball in a single shot.

8 Ball Legend
Win **10,000** games

Beat a Grandmaster
Beating a top ranked player

Underdog
Beat a player who is 3 ranks or more above you.

TITO'S TIP!
TRADITIONAL RULES APPLY... POT EITHER STRIPES OR SOLIDS AND LEAVE THE BLACK 8 BALL UNTIL LAST.

GET ALL THE ACTION OF THE POOL HALL WITHOUT LEAVING YOUR HOME!

GAMES IN THE SERIES

8 BALL QUICK FIRE POOL
Pocket as many balls as you can before the time runs out! You get a new rack of 14 balls every time you get down to the last one.

9 BALL QUICK FIRE POOL
This crazy version of the classic game is played with an extra ball! You are only allowed to strike the lowest number ball on the table! Each time you do this, you'll get 100 points.

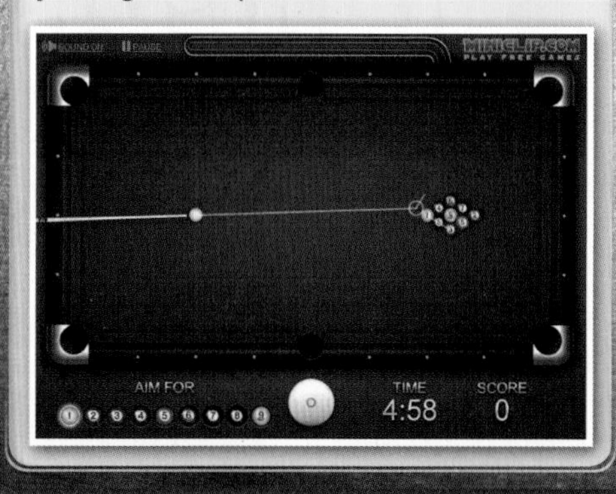

MY SCORES

High Score ....

RATE-O-METER

What do you think of 8 Ball Pool Multiplayer? Rate it by colouring the scale below.

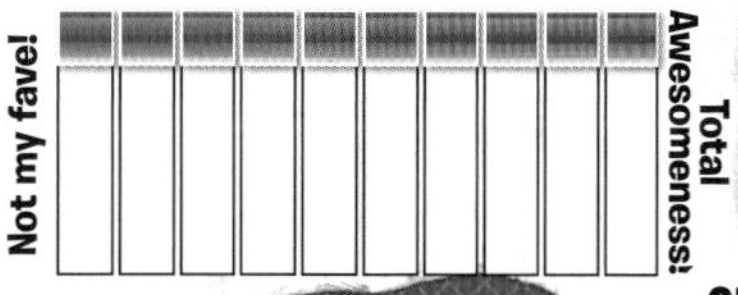

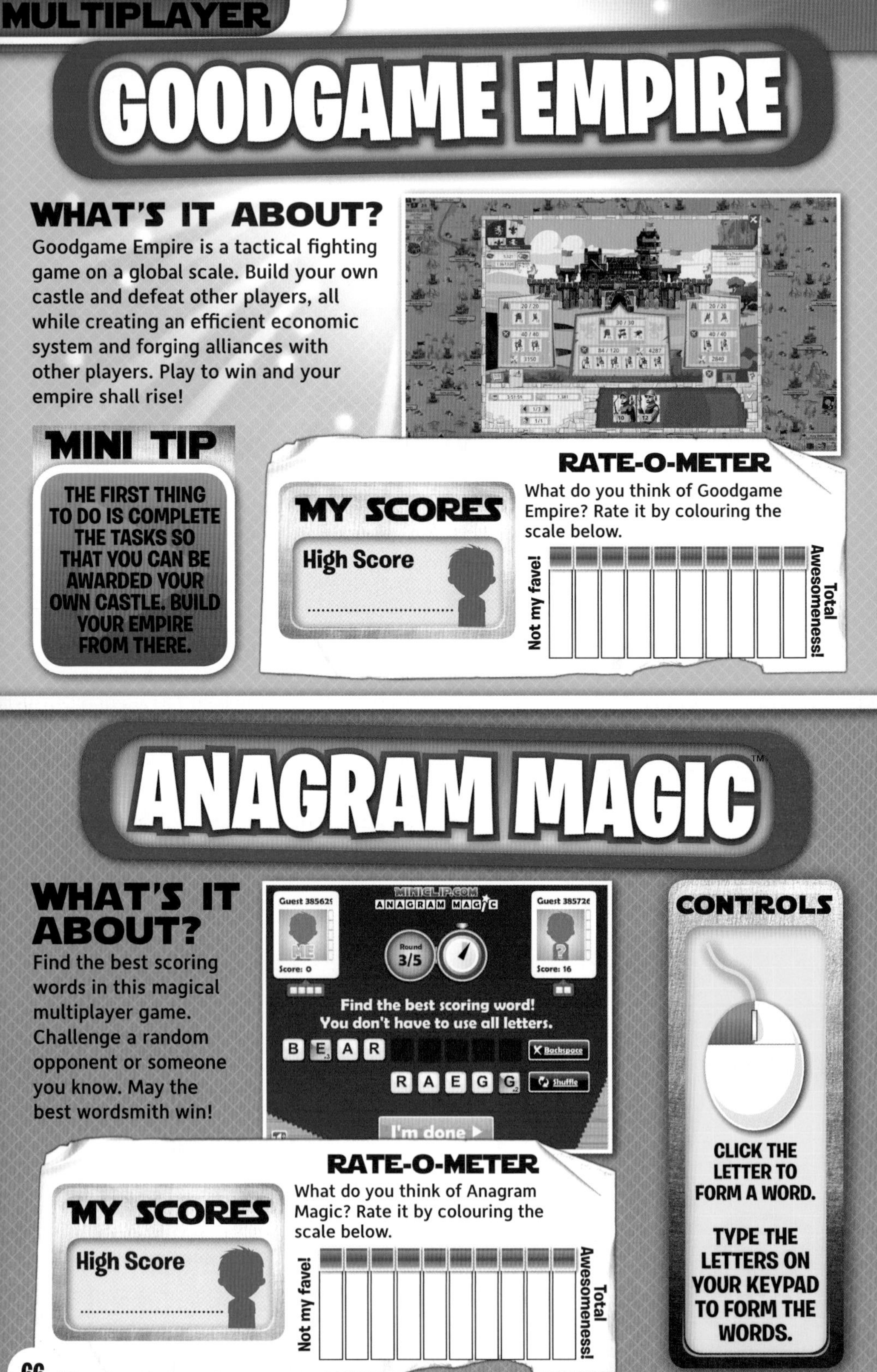

GOODGAME EMPIRE

WHAT'S IT ABOUT?

Goodgame Empire is a tactical fighting game on a global scale. Build your own castle and defeat other players, all while creating an efficient economic system and forging alliances with other players. Play to win and your empire shall rise!

MINI TIP

THE FIRST THING TO DO IS COMPLETE THE TASKS SO THAT YOU CAN BE AWARDED YOUR OWN CASTLE. BUILD YOUR EMPIRE FROM THERE.

MY SCORES

High Score

....

RATE-O-METER

What do you think of Goodgame Empire? Rate it by colouring the scale below.

Not my fave! — Total Awesomeness!

ANAGRAM MAGIC™

WHAT'S IT ABOUT?

Find the best scoring words in this magical multiplayer game. Challenge a random opponent or someone you know. May the best wordsmith win!

CONTROLS

CLICK THE LETTER TO FORM A WORD.

TYPE THE LETTERS ON YOUR KEYPAD TO FORM THE WORDS.

RATE-O-METER

What do you think of Anagram Magic? Rate it by colouring the scale below.

Not my fave! — Total Awesomeness!

MY SCORES

High Score

....

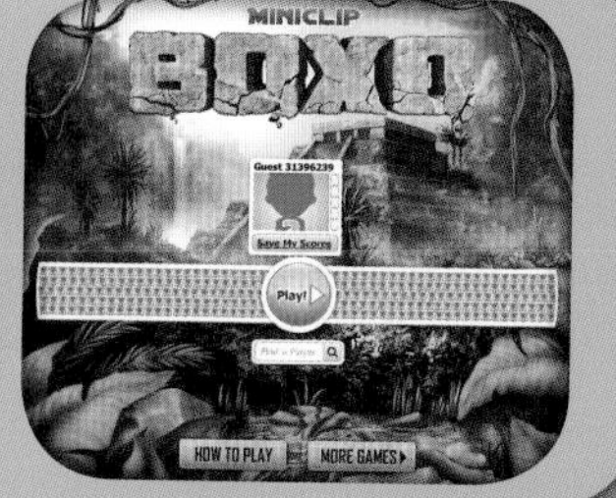

WHAT'S IT ABOUT?

It's a classic game of dots and boxes with an Mayan twist! Here, you need to use vines to create the boxes and capture gems to gain extra points.

DOTS AND BOXES ... MAYAN-STYLE!

MINI TIP

SOMETIMES IT CAN TAKE A WHILE TO GET A BOX COMPLETED. HANG ON IN THERE AND PLAY THE TACTICAL GAME. GOOD LUCK!

KIERAN'S TIP!

WATCH OUT FOR THE SKULLS! YOU'LL LOSE A POINT WHEN YOU ENCLOSE ONE.

MY SCORES

High Score

....

RATE-O-METER

What do you think of Boxo? Rate it by colouring the scale below.

Total Awesomeness!

Not my fave!

CONTROLS

PLACE VINE ON THE SIDE OF A SQUARE

AWARDS

10 — Win 10 games

100 — Win 100 games

WHAT'S IT ABOUT?

Sketch Star is an area where you can draw, animate and share your creations with all of your friends. Choose from a whole range of backgrounds and objects or simply start with a blank page and let your imagination take over. Create colourful cartoons, realistic paintings, animations, comic books and illustrations. To save time, you can even play with one of the readymade puppets. There are thousands of animations already on Sketch Star, so take a look and get inspired.

DRAW, ANIMATE AND SHARE YOUR CREATIONS!

SHARE YOUR ART

With Sketch Star, you can broadcast your artwork, attract a fanbase, send your work to friends and family or share* it on Facebook, Twitter or YouTube. Create it in your own home ... then share it with the world!

ROB'S TIP!

CHECK OUT THE AWESOME AMOUNT OF OBJECTS AND PUPPETS AVAILABLE, THERE'S SOMETHING FOR EVERY TASTE!.

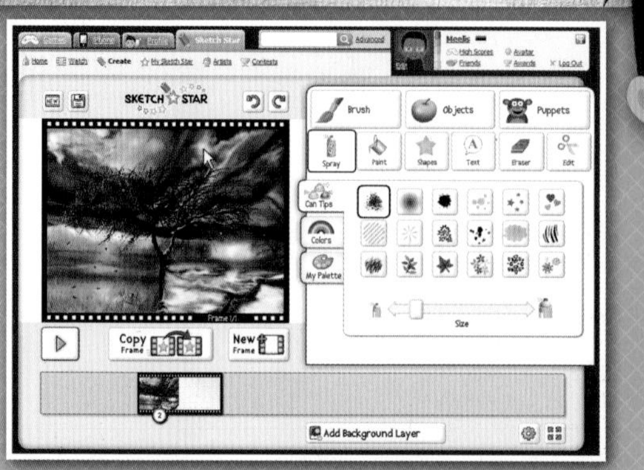

*You must be at least 13 years old to use these sites.

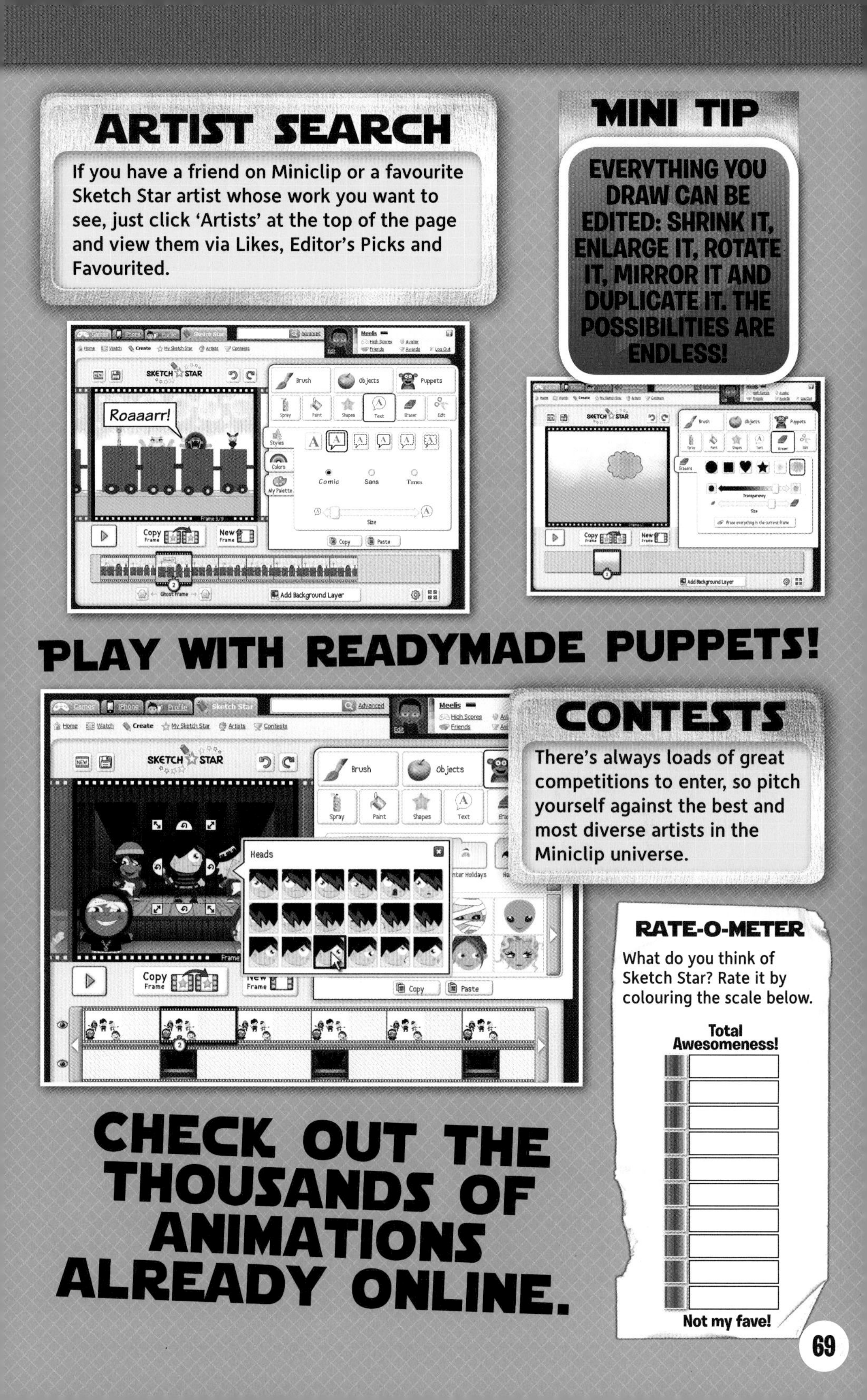

ARTIST SEARCH

If you have a friend on Miniclip or a favourite Sketch Star artist whose work you want to see, just click 'Artists' at the top of the page and view them via Likes, Editor's Picks and Favourited.

MINI TIP

EVERYTHING YOU DRAW CAN BE EDITED: SHRINK IT, ENLARGE IT, ROTATE IT, MIRROR IT AND DUPLICATE IT. THE POSSIBILITIES ARE ENDLESS!

PLAY WITH READYMADE PUPPETS!

CONTESTS

There's always loads of great competitions to enter, so pitch yourself against the best and most diverse artists in the Miniclip universe.

CHECK OUT THE THOUSANDS OF ANIMATIONS ALREADY ONLINE.

RATE-O-METER

What do you think of Sketch Star? Rate it by colouring the scale below.

Total Awesomeness!

Not my fave!

GAMES FOR MOBILE AND TABLET DEVICES

If you're on the move, check out this selection of games that can be downloaded straight to your mobile device. Now you can play anywhere you like ... so get out into the world and show everyone just how good you are!

FLING!

Fling the furballs along the lines and try to knock the other furballs of the board. The aim is to remove all the furballs (except one) to progress to the next puzzle.

MINI TIP

YOU CAN'T FLING A FURBALL STRAIGHT OFF THE BOARD. IT'S CHEATING, SO DON'T TRY IT!

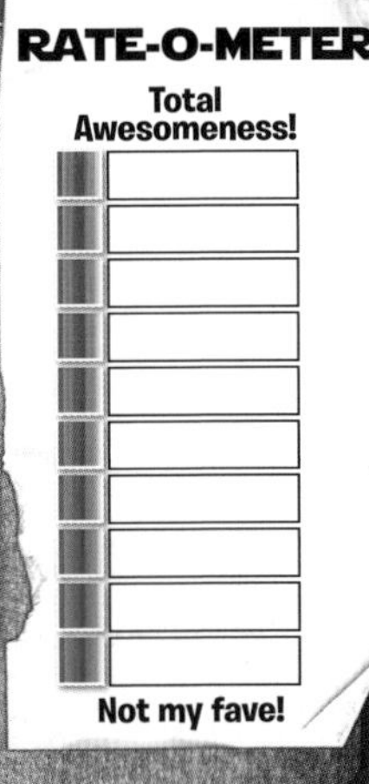

FEED THAT DRAGON

The king has ordered you to make sure the royal dragon is fed. You can do this by slinging him the food, making use of teleporters or fans.

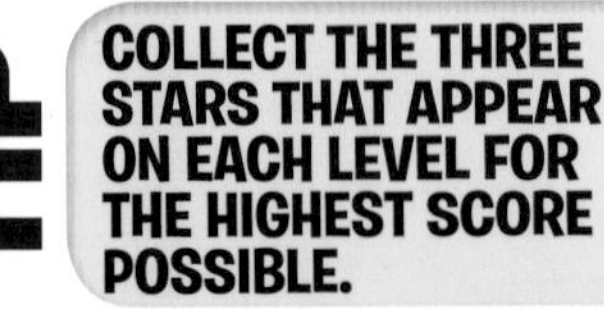

PING PONG

Seems pretty simple of the face of it... just bounce the ping pong ball as many times as you can and rack up a high score.

MINI TIP YOU CAN STILL KEEP THE BALL IN THE AIR IF IT GOES OUT OF VIEW. IT JUST BECOMES VERY HARD!

RATE-O-METER
Total Awesomeness!
Not my fave!

WORD COLLAPSE

Check spellings and spell new words to make the letter tiles disappear. The remaining tiles will the collapse and create new words.

MINI TIP DON'T JUST STEAMROLL IN... FIND THE WORDS IN THE CORRECT ORDER TO MAKE LIFE EASIER.

RATE-O-METER
Total Awesomeness!
Not my fave!

FLICK FOOTBALL

Come on, striker! Swipe your finger across the screen to curl the ball around the wall at the goal. That keeper is there to be beaten, so go and test him!

MINI TIP IT MIGHT TAKE A FEW ATTEMPTS BUT ONCE YOU GET THE PACE AND SPEED RIGHT, YOU'LL BE SCORING LEFT, RIGHT AND CENTRE!

RATE-O-METER
Not my fave!
Total Awesomeness!

AVAILABLE ON MOBILE AND TABLET DEVICES

LOOK OUT FOR THIS ICON FOR GAMES THAT ARE ALSO AVAILABLE ON MOBILE AND TABLET DEVICES.

BRYONY

PAGE 81

FAVE PUZZLE GAME:
ICE BREAKER

WHY? Axe-wielding Vikings are stranded on the ice and only you can save them!

HIGH SCORE
21,750

THERESE

PAGE 76

FAVE PUZZLE GAME:
ICE TEMPLE

WHY? I can't get enough of the mind-boggling puzzle adventures that FireBoy and WaterGirl take you on in this game.

HIGH SCORE
31,496

PAGE 79

FAVE PUZZLE GAME:
MINIPETS

WHY? Not only are the animals so cute but I can play this game on my mobile, too!

PIETER

PAGE 80

FAVE PUZZLE GAME:
SUSHI GO ROUND

WHY? Is it weird to say that I love it when the orders start to stack up and it all starts to get out of control?

HIGH SCORE
49,480

PUZZLE AND STRATEGY GAMES

Get your head in gear, because you're going to need every brain cell you have to tackle these mindblowing puzzle and strategy games. They're not about speed or dexterity, but purely about your ability to work on a problem and get the job done.

CHECK OUT A STACK OF COOL PUZZLE & STRATEGY GAMES

SNOW LINE 2

WHAT'S IT ABOUT?

Oh, no! Santa has a massive cold and his colossal sneeze has scattered the presents right across the Arctic! It's now up to you to help Mrs Claus collect the presents in time for the Christmas delivery. Draw a line to help her, then send her on her way. There's 'snow' turning back now ... Mrs Claus needs you!

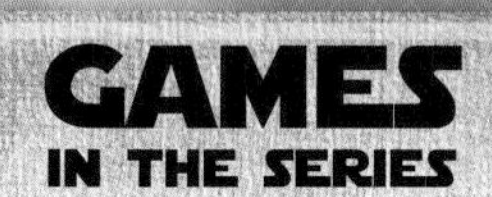

SNOW LINE

Forget helping Mrs Claus, in this game you have to help the big guy himself. Assist Santa in collecting the presents in time for Christmas Eve.

MINI TIP

MAKE SURE YOU DRAW THE LINE UNDERNEATH THE SLEIGH, OTHERWISE MRS CLAUS WILL JUST DROP TO THE GROUND.

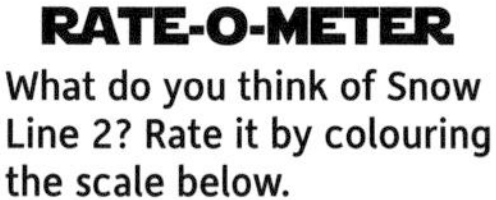

High Score

....

RATE-O-METER

What do you think of Snow Line 2? Rate it by colouring the scale below.

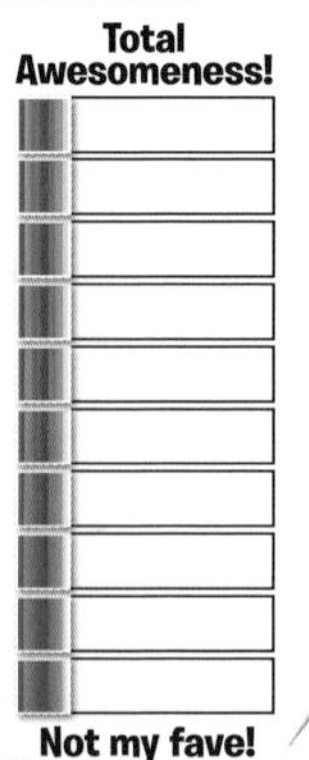

CONTROLS

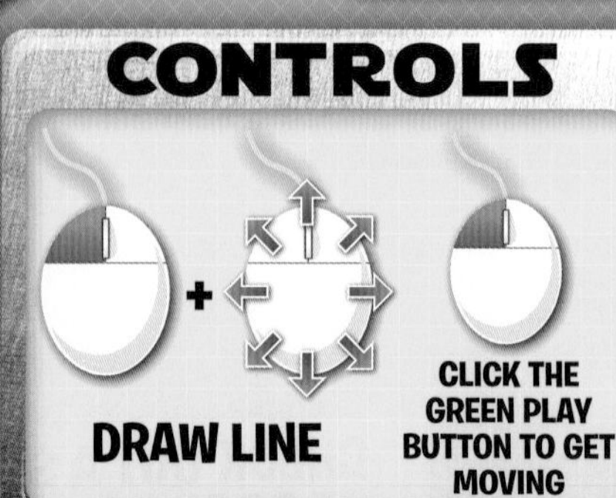

CANDY & CLYDE™

WHAT'S IT ABOUT?

Are you naughty or nice? It's up to you to decide. Choose to either help out sweet Candy or devilish Clyde in each minigame. You need to finish every minigame as quickly as you can to gain the most points possible. Get with the programme fast! The challenges will get harder as the game goes on. Good luck!

ROB'S TIP!

TIME IS TIGHT IN THESE MINIGAMES, SO MOVE QUICKLY.

ARE YOU NAUGHTY OR NICE? IT'S YOUR CHOICE!

MINI TIP

IF YOU CHOOSE CANDY, YOU'LL HAVE NICE TASKS TO COMPLETE. CLYDE WILL GIVE YOU NAUGHTY THINGS TO DO!

AWARDS

CANDY MASTER
Achieve more than **600 points** playing only as Candy.

CLYDE TROOPER
Get **600 points** playing only as Clyde to get this award.

CONTROLS

MOVE MOUSE

ACTION

RATE-O-METER

What do you think of Candy & Clyde? Rate it by colouring the scale below.

Not my fave! — Total Awesomeness!

MY SCORES

High Score ....

ICE TEMPLE

WHAT'S IT ABOUT?

Put all your plans on ice ... literally! Join FireBoy and WaterGirl and explore the Ice Temple, discovering new levels and tackling complex puzzles. Here you must operate both characters in unison to get them working as a unit. Oh, by the way, don't forget the most important part – remember to fill your pockets with blue and red diamonds as you go.

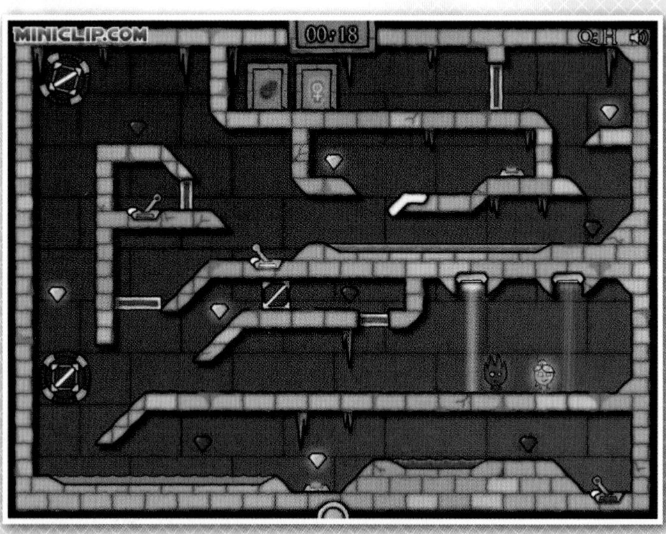

PUT YOUR PLANS ON ICE!

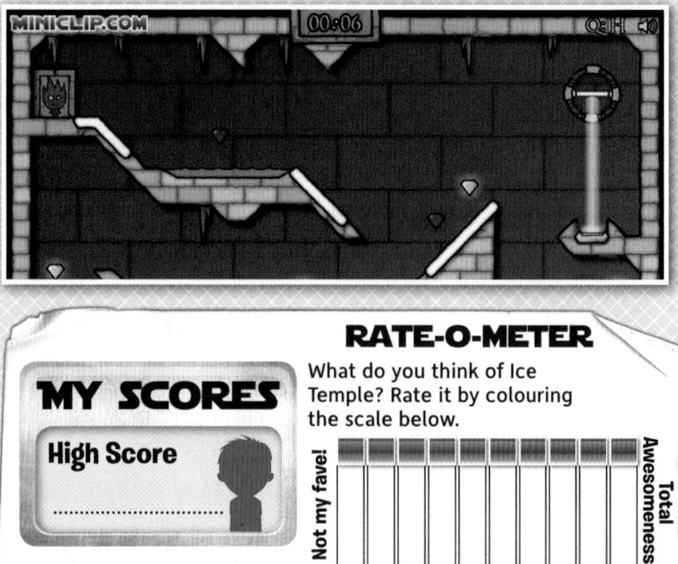

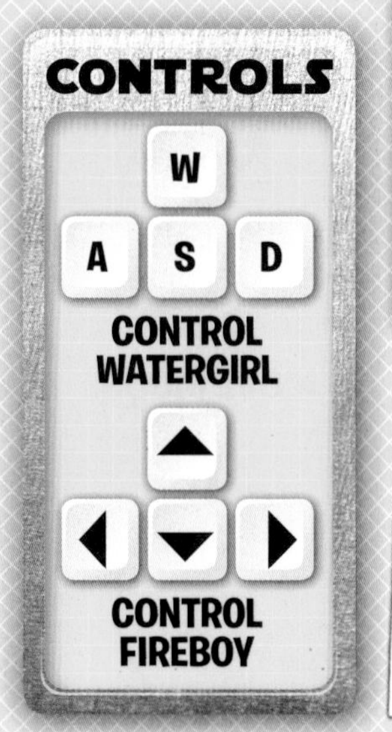

RATE-O-METER

What do you think of Ice Temple? Rate it by colouring the scale below.

Not my fave!

Total Awesomeness!

MY SCORES

High Score ....

AWARDS

ICE TEMPLE GOLD
Complete level with grade A and collect most of the diamonds available to score **30,000 points**.

ICE TEMPLE SILVER
Time is ticking but there are so many diamonds to collect! Get as many as possible and score **20,000 points**.

ICE TEMPLE BRONZE
Get WaterGirl and FireBoy working as a team and score **10,000 points**.

CREATING UNITY BETWEEN FIREBOY AND WATERGIRL IS ESSENTIAL.

MINI TIP

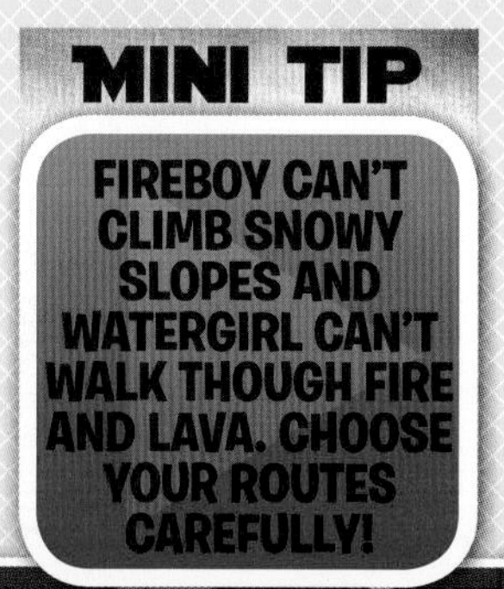

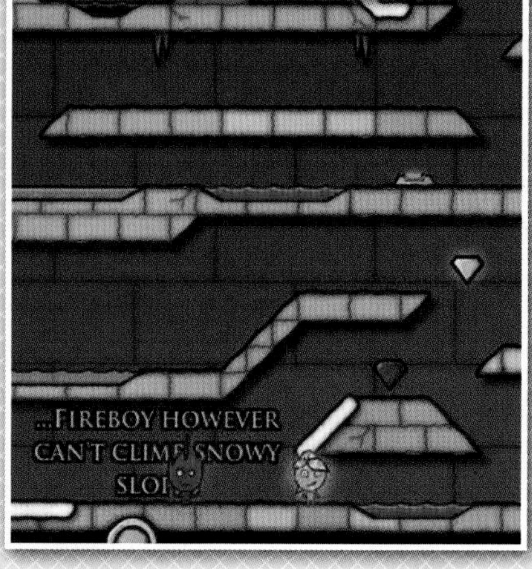

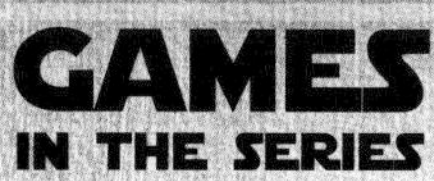

GAMES IN THE SERIES

LIGHT TEMPLE
Although this game is called Light Temple, in some levels there's no light at all. Mind your step and use the platforms to light the way.

FOREST TEMPLE
This is the first adventure to challenge FireBoy and WaterGirl. They have to complete the task and reach the exit door as fast as possible.

THERESE'S TIP!
MAKE SURE FIREBOY DOESN'T TRAVEL THROUGH WATER. IT'LL PUT OUT HIS FIRE AND END THE GAME!

THE PHARAOH'S TOMB

WHAT'S IT ABOUT?

It's another adventure with Dr Carter in this fantastic 3D game. Here he descends into an ancient Egyptian pharaoh's tomb to collect as much gold as he can. You need to help this intrepid explorer avoid monsters and traps and get out of the tomb as fast as he can. By the way ... try to keep him alive!

CONTROLS

- Arrow keys — MOVE
- A / Z — CYCLE INVENTORY
- SPACE — SELECT ITEM
- ESC — PAUSE
- TAB — MAP ON/OFF
- M — MUSIC ON/OFF
- G — GRAPHIC QUALITY

ROB'S TIP!

MIND THE HOT COALS AND KEEP CLEAR OF THE SPIKES THAT SUDDENLY APPEAR FROM BENEATH.

HELP DR CARTER AVOID MONSTERS AND TRAPS AND GET OUT OF THE TOMB ALIVE!

MINI TIP

LOOK OUT FOR THE HEALING POTIONS. DRINK THEM TO HEAL WOUNDS.

MY SCORES

High Score ....

RATE-O-METER

What do you think of Pharaoh's Tomb? Rate it by colouring the scale below.

Not my fave! — Total Awesomeness!

AVAILABLE ON MOBILE AND TABLET DEVICES

WHAT'S IT ABOUT?

This free app game lets you build your own animal shelter for some of the cutest animals around. You have to make them comfortable in their new accommodation, arrange for the animals to go on dates and watch them as they fall in love. Not only that, when their babies arrive, it's your job to care for them too. You can hire caretakers to help you out, but you're in charge of the friendliest animal shelter around.

WELCOME TO THE WORLD'S FRIENDLIEST ANIMAL SHELTER.

MORE IN STORE

- DECORATE AND PERSONALISE YOUR SHELTER.
- COMPLETE QUESTS TO EARN REWARDS.
- LEVEL UP AND UNLOCK OVER 60 ANIMALS.
- EARN REVENUE BY SELLING VIA YOUR SHOP AND VENDING CART.

SERGIO'S TIP!

ONCE TWO ANIMALS FALL IN LOVE, BUY A CRADLE AND PREPARE FOR THE NEW ARRIVAL!

High Score

....

RATE-O-METER

What do you think of Mini Pets? Rate it by colouring the scale below.

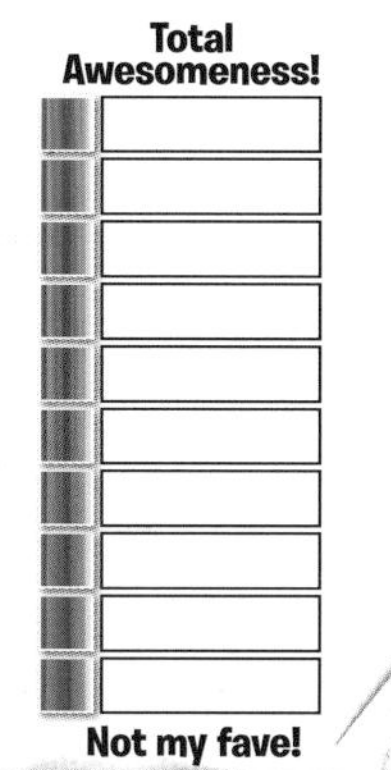

MINI TIP

THE MORE YOU IMPROVE YOUR SHELTER, THE MORE ANIMALS IT WILL HOUSE.

74,146
2
3 / 3
TAP TO INAUGURATE
Decorate your shelter

SUSHI GO ROUND

WHAT'S IT ABOUT?

Out with the old and in with the new! You are the replacement chef at a sushi restaurant, but there's a catch ... you're on a 1-week trial. You must create the correct recipes and serve the hungry customers their orders with only a recipe book to help you. The conveyor belts never stop moving and the customers never stop coming, so there's no chance of a rest!

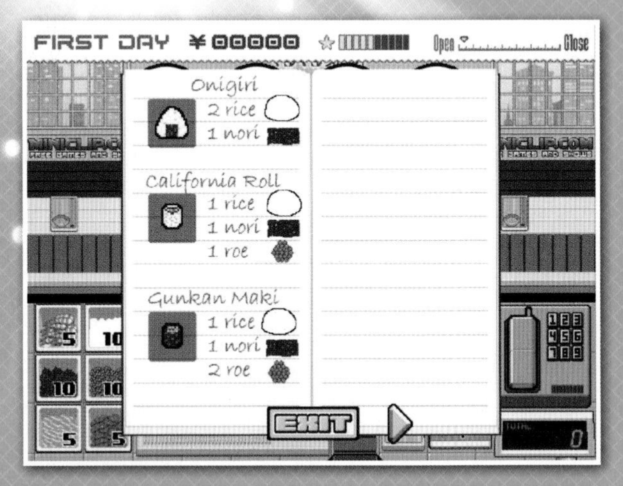

CREATE THE CORRECT RECIPES AND SERVE THE HUNGRY CUSTOMERS!

MY SCORES

High Score

....

RATE-O-METER

What do you think of Sushi Go Round? Rate it by colouring the scale below.

Total Awesomeness!

Not my fave!

PIETER'S TIP!

MEMORISE THE SUSHI COMBOS AND YOU'LL GET MUCH QUICKER AT HELPING CUSTOMERS!

MINI TIP

GET WORKING THE MOMENT YOUR FIRST CUSTOMER ARRIVES. IF YOU'RE SLOW OFF THE MARK, YOU'LL END UP IN BIG TROUBLE.

CONTROLS

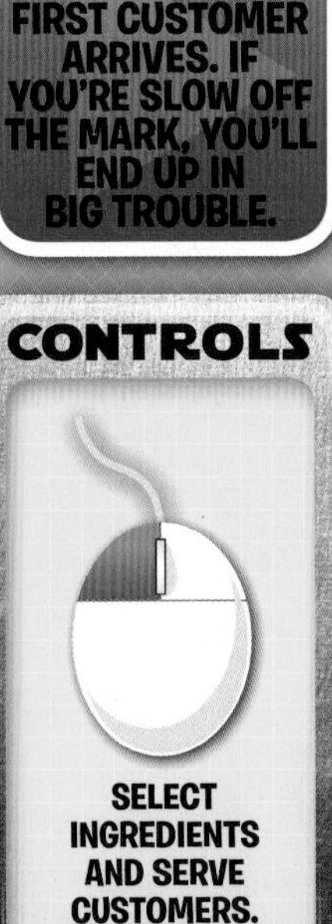

SELECT INGREDIENTS AND SERVE CUSTOMERS.

WHAT'S IT ABOUT?

The Vikings need to get back to their ship, but they are frozen in an icy cavern. You need to slash the ice with your axe and send the frozen Vikings plummeting back to their ship. However, some of them will still be stuck inside a gigantic icicle. Luckily, there's a mean Viking onboard ready to smash the ice and release his comrades from their frozen prison.

MINI TIP

FILL IN LARGE GAPS IN THE ICE BY SLASHING THE HUGE ICICLES ABOVE.

MY SCORES

High Score ....

RATE-O-METER

What do you think of Ice Breaker? Rate it by colouring the scale below.

Not my fave! — Total Awesomeness!

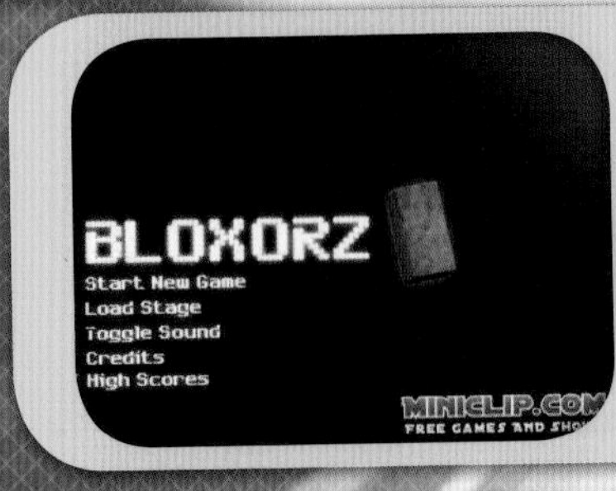

WHAT'S IT ABOUT?

Seems easy enough ... just get the block to fall into the square hole and you'll move to the next level. But as the levels advance, the game gets harder. There are switches and bridges to bring into play as you move the block around the tiles. There are also teleporter switches that take your block to another level and split it in two at the same time.

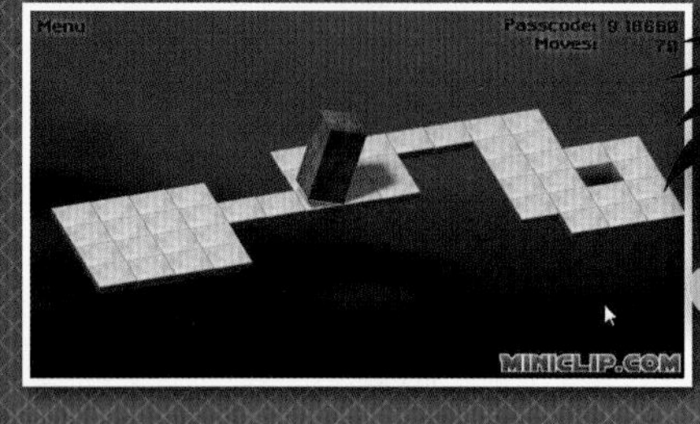

THIS GAME WILL KNOCK YOU BLOCKS OFF!

MINI TIP

BE CAREFUL NOT TO FALL OFF THE EDGE AND WATCH OUT FOR THE ORANGE TILES ... THEY'RE VERY FRAGILE.

RATE-O-METER

What do you think of Bloxorz? Rate it by colouring the scale below.

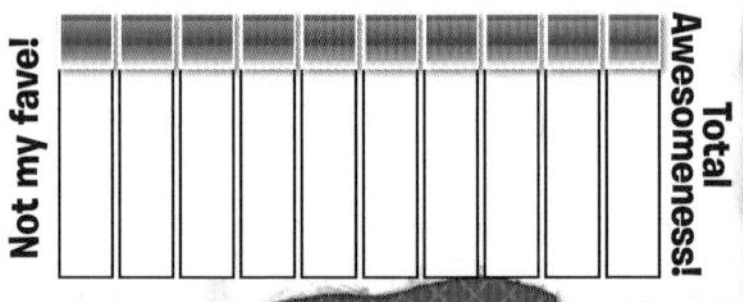

WHAT'S IT ABOUT?

Bomba is a little green creature, and it's your job to guide him though the stars, lighting them up along the way. Make sure you don't touch the walls, rotating cogs or any of the moving objects or Bomba will explode. But Bomba isn't the only exploding thing in this game – there are bombs to help him blast his way through obstacles. Good luck!

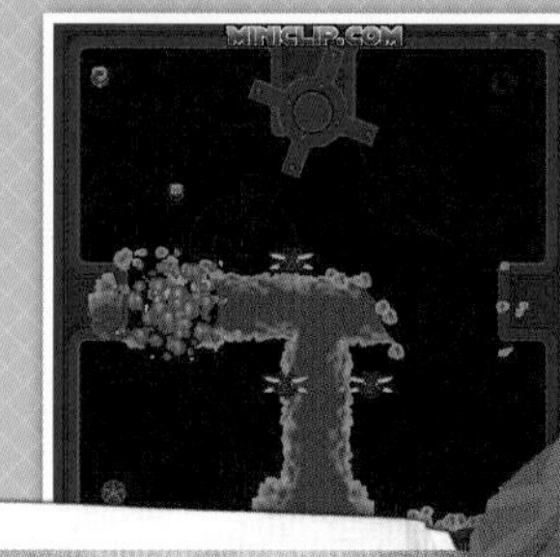

ROB'S TIP!

WATCH OUT FOR WATER. IF YOU STAY IN IT TOO LONG, YOU WON'T SURVIVE.

MY SCORES

High Score ....

RATE-O-METER

What do you think of Bomba? Rate it by colouring the scale below.

Total Awesomeness!

Not my fave!

BOMBA'S ON A MISSION TO AVOID THE COGS AND LIGHT THE STARS.

KEEPING UP WITH MINICLIP

It's easy to keep up-to-date with what's going on at Miniclip. You can talk about games with your mates or discover when a new game is due to be launched. Here's how to do it!

YOU MUST BE AT LEAST 13 YEARS OLD TO USE THESE SITES.

FACEBOOK

The Miniclip page on Facebook is a great base for getting all the latest news, info and updates from our universe. You can trade gaming tips with other users and see what friends really think of the games. Plus, watch this space for any announcements.

WWW.FACEBOOK.COM/MINICLIP

TWITTER

Twitter will literally keep you up to the second with what's going on. Join @Miniclip and other fans to tweet about the best games, insider tips and anything #miniclip that crosses your mind. Start topics, join in current discussions or ask for gaming help. Whatever you do, you're bound to get a quick answer here!

WWW.TWITTER.COM/MINICLIP

YOU TUBE

There's loads of recorded gameplay on YouTube. Here you can type in the name of your favourite game and watch someone else playing through the levels. This can help show you the way out of a tight spot if you're having trouble progressing past a certain point.

WWW.YOUTUBE.COM/USER/MINICLIP

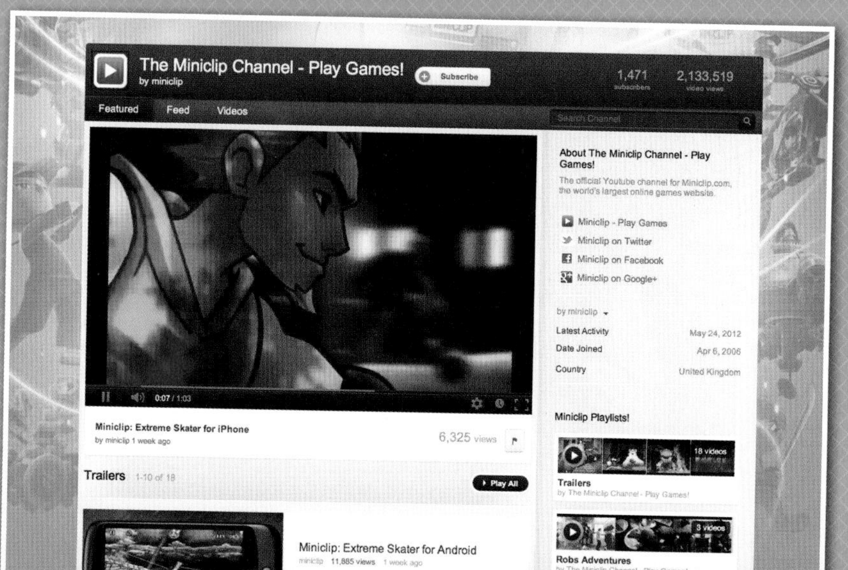

BEN

PAGE 96

FAVE STUNT GAME:
TRIALS MOUNTAIN HEIGHTS

WHY? It's amazing how real this game looks! The courses are brilliant and very addictive.

HIGH SCORE
2:13 TIME

ROB L.

PAGE 90

FAVE STUNT GAME:
ISTUNT 2

WHY? I love snowboarding and can do way more tricks in this game than I can in real life. It hurts a lot less whan I crash, too!

THERESE

PAGE 92

FAVE STUNT GAME:
STUNT PILOT 2

WHY? Piloting that little stunt plane can be frustrating, exhilarating and just 'plane' fun all at the same time!

XIAOMAN

PAGE 94

FAVE STUNT GAME:
GRAVITY GUY

WHY? Staying alert the whole time you are playing this game is important. If you don't, it's over pretty fast!

STUNT GAMES

Catch some air in this ultimate collection of stunt games. Whether you're into motocross, jet skiing, free running or skateboarding, this zone is ready and waiting for you to unleash your tricks. No need for a helmet and pads here though ... play from the safety of your sofa!

CHECK OUT A STACK OF INSANE STUNT GAMES

EXTREME SKATER™

WHAT'S IT ABOUT?

This is one heck of a skateboard ride. Travel at colossal speed through a series of rough and ready courses to put your gaming skate skills to the test. Collect the coins and throw in some midair tricks to gains bonuses. But make sure you get your balance for a perfect landing or you'll be in big trouble.

CONTROLS

◀ ▶ LEFT AND RIGHT TO TILT IN MIDAIR

Z X C DO TRICKS

▲ ▼ UP TO JUMP& DOWN TO CROUCH

ROB'S TIP!

DO AS MANY TURNS AS YOU CAN IN THE AIR TO GAIN EXTRA COMBO POINTS. LOOK OUT FOR THE CAUTION SIGNS.

TRAVEL AT COLOSSAL SPEED AND PUT YOUR SKATE SKILLS TO THE TEST!

MINI TIP

THE CONTROLS ARE BASIC TO START WITH, SO LOOK OUT FOR THE BONUS MOVES AS YOU PROGRESS THROUGH THE LEVELS.

MY SCORES

High Score

....

RATE-O-METER

What do you think of Extreme Skater? Rate it by colouring the scale below.

Not my fave! — Total Awesomeness!

WHAT'S IT ABOUT?

Take to the arena and head through a series of tough obstacle courses on a motocross bike. This game is all about balance and agility to hop between platforms and stay onboard your ride. There's some high-flying hurdles to overcome here, so only the ultimate crowd pleaser will progress through the levels. Hit the accelerator, watch the clock and make sure your crash helmet is tightly secured!

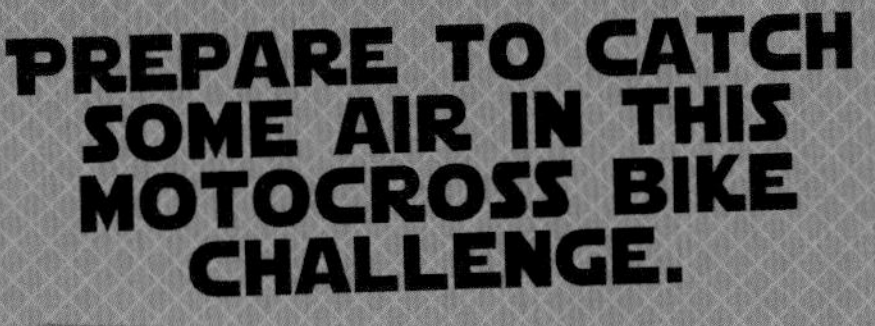

RATE-O-METER

What do you think of Trial Bike Pro? Rate it by colouring the scale below.

Total Awesomeness!

Not my fave!

CONTROLS

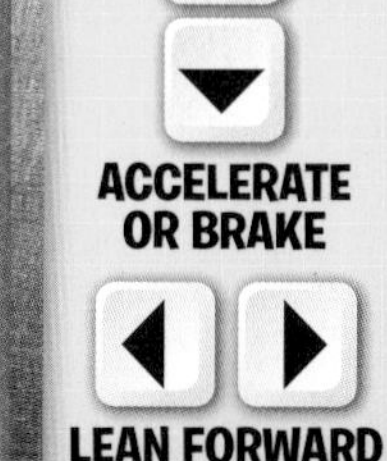

ACCELERATE OR BRAKE

LEAN FORWARD OR BACK

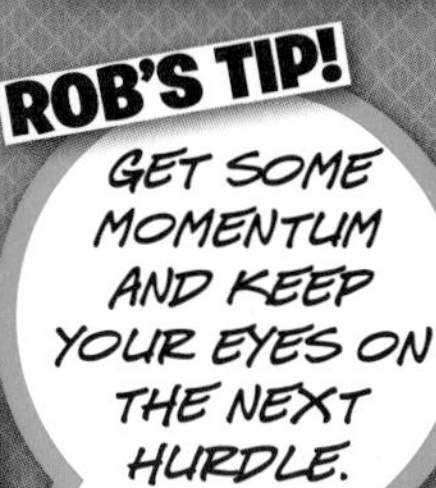

GAMES IN THE SERIES

TRIAL BIKE

Navigate the jaw-dropping obstacles in the quickest possible time.

iSTUNT 2™

AVAILABLE ON MOBILE AND TABLET DEVICES

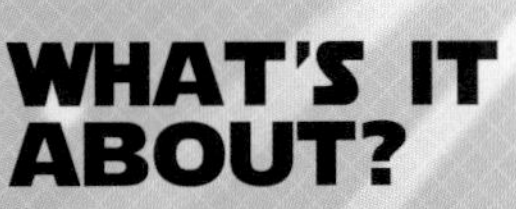

WHAT'S IT ABOUT?

Grab your snowboard, strap on your goggles and head for the slopes! It's time to get up to full speed and pull off some daring extreme stunts. The idea is to pull off as many awesome tricks as possible because each one gains you points. Crouch, jump, turn and spin through the most awesome snowboard run ... ever!

ROB L.'S TIP!

MAKE SURE YOUR TRICK FINISHES BEFORE YOU GET TOO CLOSE TO THE GROUND – OTHERWISE IT'S BRUISE-A-RAMA!

SNOWBOARD AT THE READY ... IT'S TIME TO BECOME AN ISTUNT 2 LEGEND!

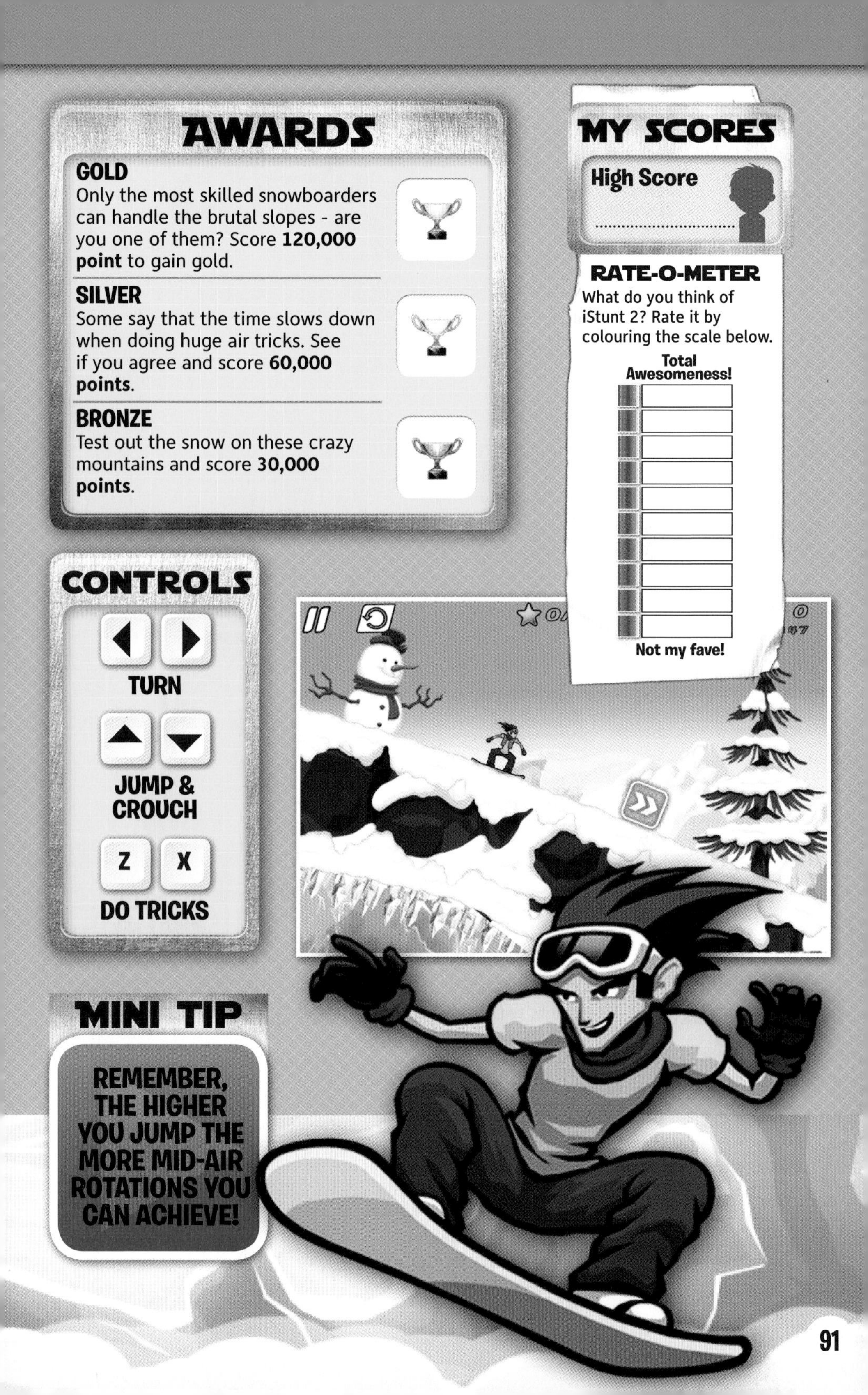

AWARDS

GOLD
Only the most skilled snowboarders can handle the brutal slopes - are you one of them? Score **120,000 point** to gain gold.

SILVER
Some say that the time slows down when doing huge air tricks. See if you agree and score **60,000 points**.

BRONZE
Test out the snow on these crazy mountains and score **30,000 points**.

MY SCORES

High Score ....

RATE-O-METER

What do you think of iStunt 2? Rate it by colouring the scale below.

Total Awesomeness!

Not my fave!

CONTROLS

TURN

JUMP & CROUCH

Z X

DO TRICKS

MINI TIP

REMEMBER, THE HIGHER YOU JUMP THE MORE MID-AIR ROTATIONS YOU CAN ACHIEVE!

STUNT PILOT 2

WHAT'S IT ABOUT?

This is the long-awaited sequel to one of the best stunt pilot games around. Get comfortable in the cockpit and prepare for some amazing stunts. There are rings to fly through and paths to follow to complete the levels. If you're feeling daring, you can even zip through the course on turbo! It's time for take-off, pilot ace!

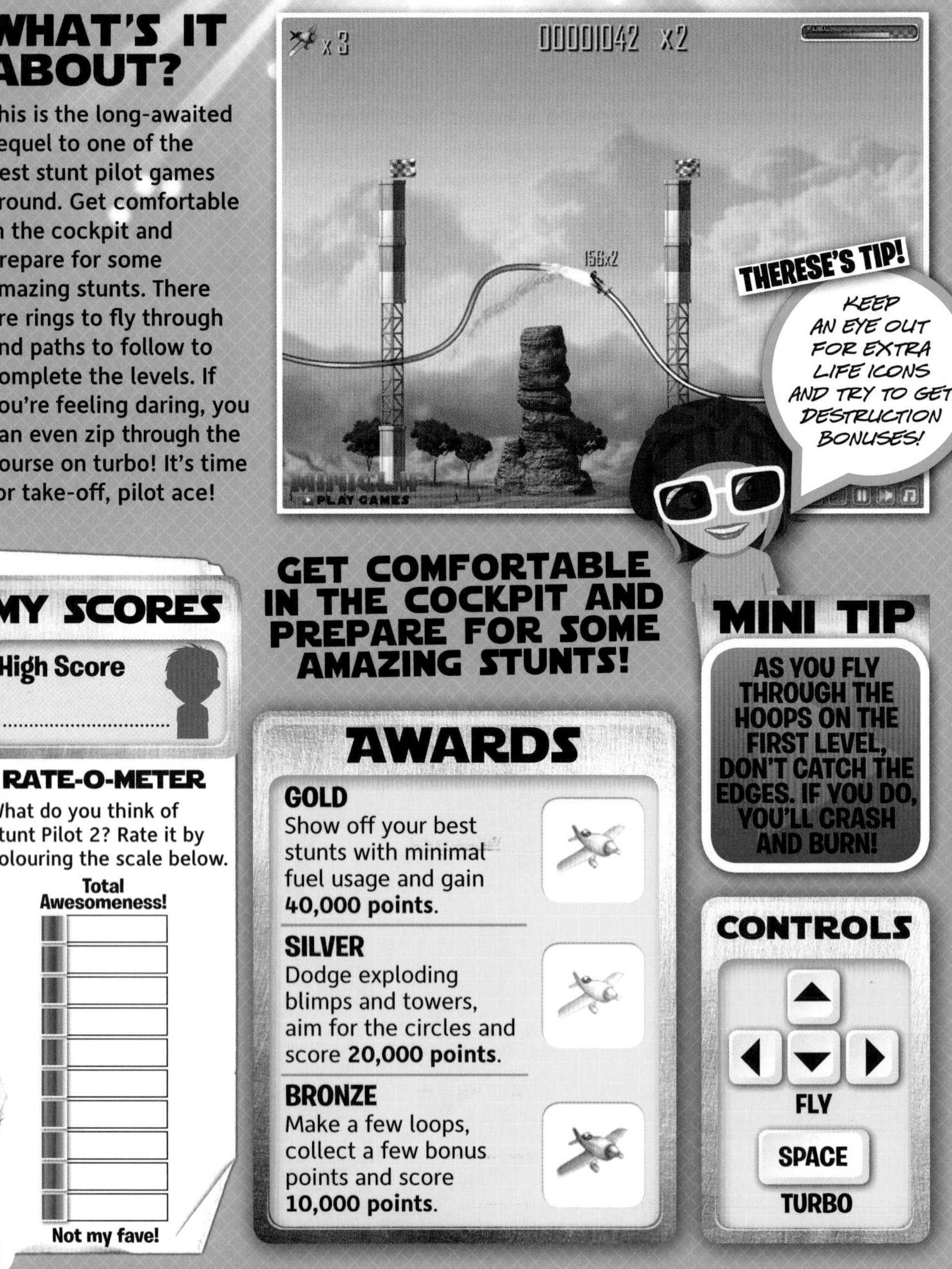

THERESE'S TIP!

KEEP AN EYE OUT FOR EXTRA LIFE ICONS AND TRY TO GET DESTRUCTION BONUSES!

MY SCORES

High Score

....

RATE-O-METER

What do you think of Stunt Pilot 2? Rate it by colouring the scale below.

Total Awesomeness!

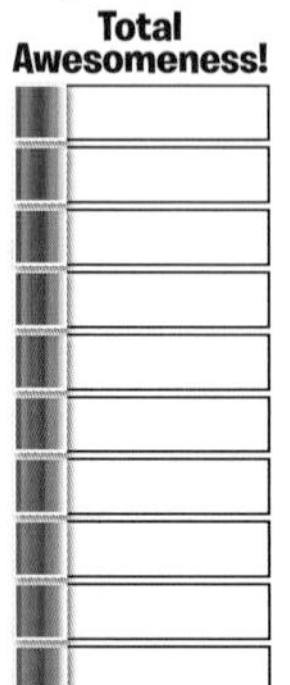

Not my fave!

GET COMFORTABLE IN THE COCKPIT AND PREPARE FOR SOME AMAZING STUNTS!

AWARDS

GOLD
Show off your best stunts with minimal fuel usage and gain **40,000 points.**

SILVER
Dodge exploding blimps and towers, aim for the circles and score **20,000 points.**

BRONZE
Make a few loops, collect a few bonus points and score **10,000 points.**

MINI TIP

AS YOU FLY THROUGH THE HOOPS ON THE FIRST LEVEL, DON'T CATCH THE EDGES. IF YOU DO, YOU'LL CRASH AND BURN!

CONTROLS

FLY – arrow keys

SPACE – **TURBO**

TG MOTOCROSS 3

WHAT'S IT ABOUT?

It's a dirt bike extravaganza like no other. Rev the engine, hit the trail and prepare for a rough ride. Tackle the slopes, bottomless ravines and underground tunnels armed only with a motocross bike and your skill. This game is all about balance and precision, throw in some freestyle tricks and you're on your way to becoming a TG Motocross 3 star!

AWARDS

GOLD
Get to the final finish line with a total score **200,000 points** or more.

SILVER
Treat the terrain with respect and score **100,000 points**.

BRONZE
Take on one of the toughest dirt bike courses and score **50,000 points**.

ROB'S TIP!
TRY THROWING IN SOME TRICKS AS YOU JUMP – YOUR POINTS TOTAL WILL ROCKET.

MY SCORES

High Score

....

RATE-O-METER
What do you think of TG Motocross 3? Rate it by colouring the scale below.

Total Awesomeness!

Not my fave!

REV THE ENGINE, HIT THE TRAIL AND CATCH SOME AIR!

CONTROLS

▲ ◀ ▼ ▶ DRIVE

Z X C V B DO TRICKS

GRAVITY GUY™

WHAT'S IT ABOUT?

You control gravity to outrun your pursuer in this space-age game. Flip gravity to either the ground or the ceiling and make it through each level. You can also play a multiplayer version of the game where you race against your friends. This game will turn your world upside down and back again.

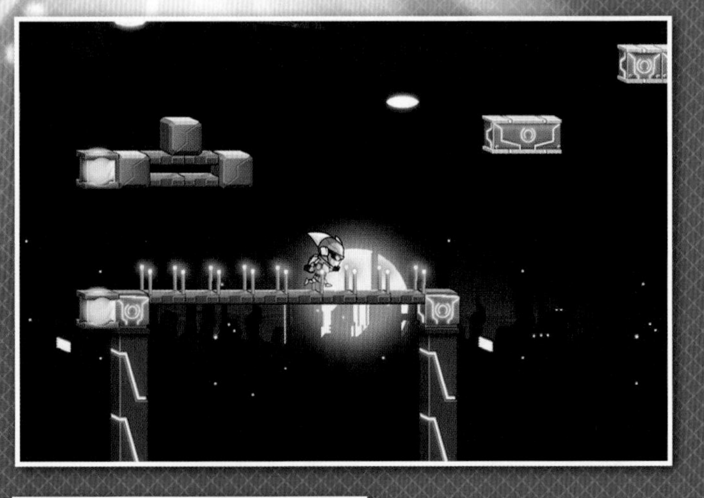

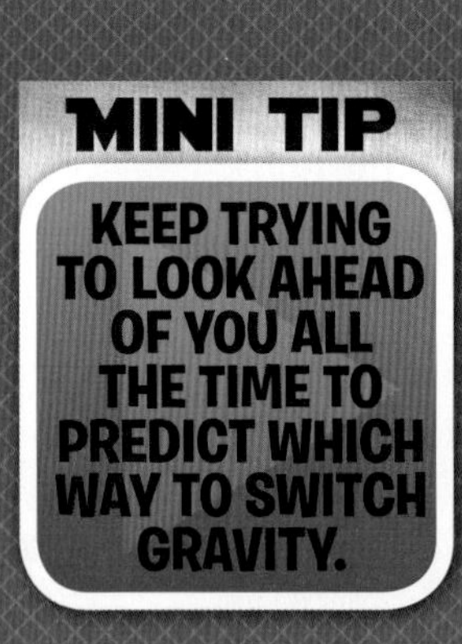

LET THE GRAVITY GAMES BEGIN!

AWARDS

GOLD
Use your skills to trap and slow down your pursuer and score **35,000 points**.

SILVER
Precision is the skill for survival. Score **25,000 points** to gain Silver.

BRONZE
You've been granted the power to control gravity, use it to get **15,000 points**.

AS THE LEVELS ADVANCE, SEE IF YOU CAN TRAP YOUR PURSUER AND TAKE HIM OUT OF THE GAME!

MY SCORES

High Score

....

RATE-O-METER

What do you think of Gravity Guy? Rate it by colouring the scale below.

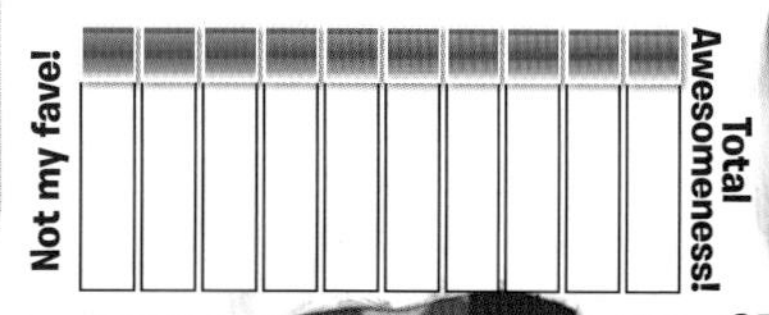

TRIALS MOUNTAIN HEIGHTS

WHAT'S IT ABOUT?

This dirt bike skill game has great gameplay mixed with realistic backgrounds. As the name suggests, you take your bike on a trial to drive across mountain terrain, keeping perfect balance at all times. Every time you crash, you'll incur a penalty so making the right lean at the correct time is crucial. Rev it up and get biking!

CONTROLS

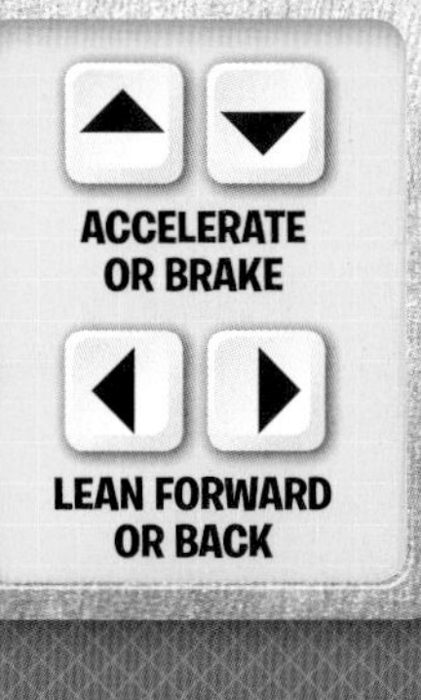

ACCELERATE OR BRAKE

LEAN FORWARD OR BACK

MINI TIP

ROB'S TIP!

REV IT UP AND GET BIKING!

GAMES IN THE SERIES

TRIALS 2

Navigate over obstacles and obstructions in the quickest time possible.

TRIALS CONSTRUCTION YARD

Head to the building site to pull off your motocross tricks in the danger of a construction yard.

TRIALS DYNAMITE

In a bizarre twist, you have to try to inflict as much damage as possible on the driver to gain points. Poor guy!

MY SCORES

High Score

....

RATE-O-METER

What do you think of Trials Mountain Heights? Rate it by colouring the scale below.

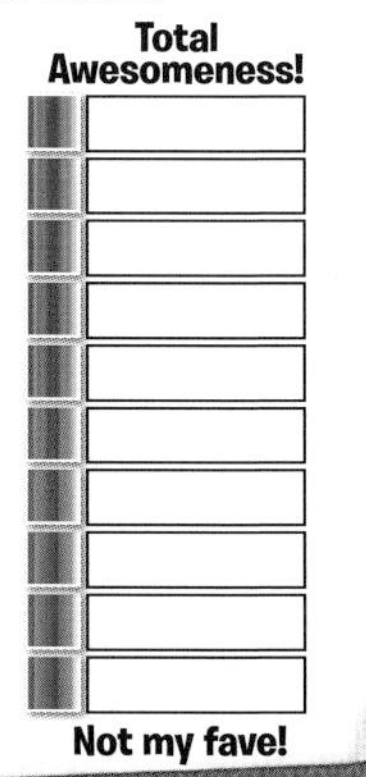

DEVELOPER Q&A

Name: Damien Clarke
Age: 24
Lives: Melbourne, Australia

DAMIEN DEVELOPED HIS FIRST GAME AT AGE 14

How did you get started in game development?

When I was growing up, I used to draw mazes on paper and my brother would play by moving his finger around the page, pretending to be the character and opening and closing pretend doors. By the time I got to high school, some of the computers had a copy of Flash 4 and I quickly realised that you could not only make animations, but make them interactive as well. By that point, I was hooked and spent years learning how to make more and more complex things.

What's the hardest thing about game development?

Finishing them! Games can take a long time to make, and it's so easy to get a quarter of the way through and run out of steam. Something I try really hard to do now is finish all the projects I start. This often means working through a dull patch to get to the next exciting part. Finished is always better than perfect – always!

What game are you most proud of?

Bloxorz. It has a very stupid name, but it just seemed to work as a game. I didn't need to force it to make the levels work. It's the only one I've made that people try to copy all the time, so it must have worked!

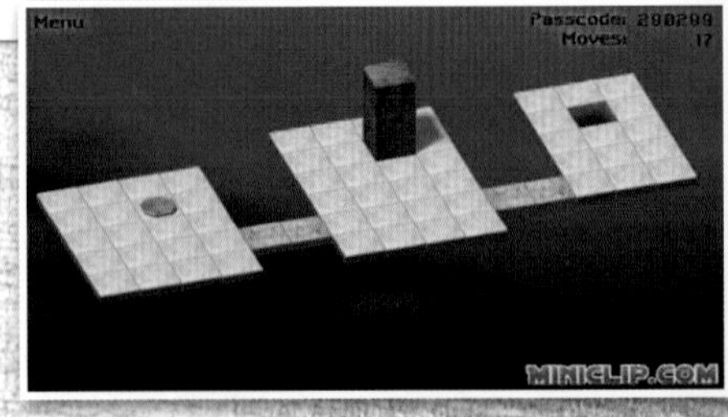

What's your favourite game on Miniclip (not made by you)?

Acno's Energizer! I used to love that game. Acno's energizer and Soap Bubble were my two biggest influences when I first began.

What's your favourite game of all time?

Abe's Oddysee and Abe's Exoddus - I can't choose one over the other, both are fantastic. They seemed to create a whole universe and then only let you see a small part of it, it just felt like such a huge place.

How many people in your team/studio? What do they do?

Just me. Which means I get to do all the code, maths, art, animation, gameplay, story, level design, everything! Games combine so many different skills, which, for me, is why they're so appealing to work on. Also, working on my own means I don't have to argue with anyone, but the downside is that things can take a very long time to finish, especially if you have school or uni and a job that keeps taking up your time. I should probably go and find a team!

Where do you get your ideas for games?

I'm not sure. Once I was rolling a 9-volt battery around a tabletop. Another time I wondered what it'd be like to fill a old brick garden up with water. Another time I looked through a postal tube and imagined myself zooming through it. Ideas are everywhere, and the good ideas always stand out.

What advice would you give someone who wanted to work in games?

If you want to make the games look cool, make the characters lovable or disgusting, or make them tell a story, then get drawing! Learn how to animate and see if you like it. Play with Photoshop or try a 3D program. There are so many different directions you can go within the artistic side of games that it's definitely worth exploring.

Anything else?

Just make the games interactive and fun, then do your maths!

SEE OTHER DEVELOPER Q&As ON PAGES 126, 127, 154 AND 155

ALEXANDER

PAGE 103

FAVE SEASONAL GAME:
MOBY DICK 2

WHY? Where else can you be a 200-ton whale destroying and eating everything in sight? Nowhere, that's where!

HIGH SCORE
19,583,050

JANE

PAGE 104

FAVE SEASONAL GAME:
ACID FACTORY

WHY? It's great fun trying to navigate your way around the factory, helping Harry and avoiding those zombies!

SERGIO

PAGE 107

FAVE SEASONAL GAME:
MONSTER ISLAND

WHY? Trying to conquer this land of monsters is a blast! Its survival of the fittest at its very best.

XIAOMAN

PAGE 106

FAVE SEASONAL GAME:
SKYWIRE

WHY? This game lets me live on the edge without going near it. I'm glad the passengers aren't real as well!

SEASONAL GAMES

'Tis the season to be jolly ... excited! These seasonal games cover every part of the year from springtime to Christmas. This section is a mix of all kinds of games, so take a look – like a lucky dip, you never know what you're going to find!

CHECK OUT A STACK OF WICKED SEASONAL GAMES

MONKEY LANDER

WHAT'S IT ABOUT?

This game has it all... monkeys, bananas and a spaceship! You have to help this crazy jungle creature collect all the bananas before landing safely on the platform of each level. Look out for bonuses, fuel and extra lives, too. They'll all be disguised as different types of fruit.

CONTROLS

MOVE

A MONKEY IN A SPACESHIP? THAT'S MONKEY MADNESS!

MINI TIP

MAKE SURE YOU LAND THE SPACESHIP SOFTLY ONTO THE PLATFORM. IF IT'S TOO FAST, YOU'LL CRASH.

MY SCORES

High Score

....

RATE-O-METER

What do you think of Monkey Lander? Rate it by colouring the scale below.

Not my fave! — Total Awesomeness!

MOBY DICK 2

WHAT'S IT ABOUT?

This is a whale of a game with a big appetite! Believe it or not, you play the part of the white whale in this epic adventure, and you're always hungry! It's your job to destroy ships and eat everything that moves. Most importantly though ... stay alive as long as you can. Check out why this game's creating a real splash!

AWARDS

FISH TERROR AWARD
Chomp down 150 fish to gain this award.

WAVE AWARD
Survive and beat wave 20 to get this award.

ACHIEVEMENTS AWARD
Get 36 achievements throughout the game to win this award!

MY SCORES

High Score

....

RATE-O-METER

What do you think of Moby Dick 2? Rate it by colouring the scale below.

Total Awesomeness!

Not my fave!

CONTROLS

MOVE

BOOST

ALEXANDER'S TIP!

KEEP AWAY FROM NETS, HARPOONS AND CANNONBALLS. THEY'RE NO GOOD FOR YOUR HEALTH!

GAMES IN THE SERIES

MOBY DICK
Play this original version of the game. It's similar to Moby Dick 2, but with a few different challenges.

WHAT'S IT ABOUT?

Yikes! Toxichem Inc's Acid Factory is totally flooded with acid. Luckily, some of the floor is still above the flood level. Help factory worker Harry escape the deadly liquid, as well as some pretty gruesome-looking enemies! Collect all the batteries to power the portal and get to the next sector. Navigate Harry safely without falling into the nasty green stuff or bumping into the even nastier monsters!

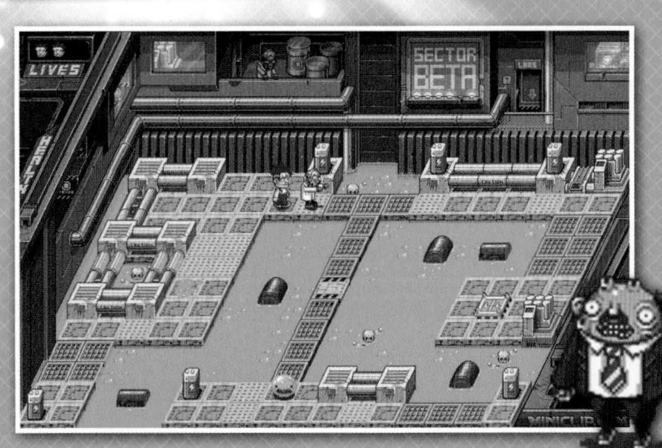

THE ACID FACTORY IS TOTALLY FLOODED WITH NASTY GREEN STUFF! YIKES!

MY SCORES

RATE-O-METER

What do you think of Acid Factory? Rate it by colouring the scale below.

Total Awesomeness!

Not my fave!

POLAR JUMP

WHAT'S IT ABOUT?

This polar bear is the most gravity-defying creature on the planet. Just click on him to make him jump as high as possible. How far will he go? Once he's up and away, just keep clicking on him to take blast into the stratosphere. Be careful though ... this bear drops as fast as he jumps!

AWARDS

GALACTIC BEAR
Jump all the way into space and reach **10,000** metres.

SPACE BEAR
Help the Polar bear reach **3,000** metres.

POLAR JUMP CHRISTMAS AWARD
Score **2,500 points** to get this award.

CONTROLS

JUMP

SPACE

DEPLOY PARACHUTE (ONCE COLLECTED)

ROB'S TIP!

TRY TO JUMP THE BEAR THROUGH THE ICONS TO GAIN PARACHUTES AND OTHER BONUSES.

MINI TIP

WATCH THE ARROW - IT WILL GIVE YOU AN IDEA WHERE THE BEAR IS GOING TO DROP.

MY SCORES

High Score ....

RATE-O-METER

What do you think of Polar Jump? Rate it by colouring the scale below.

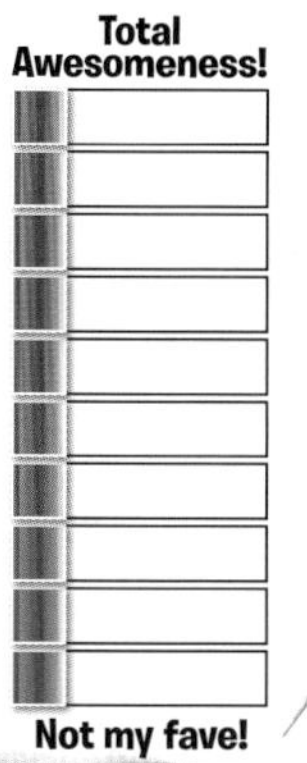

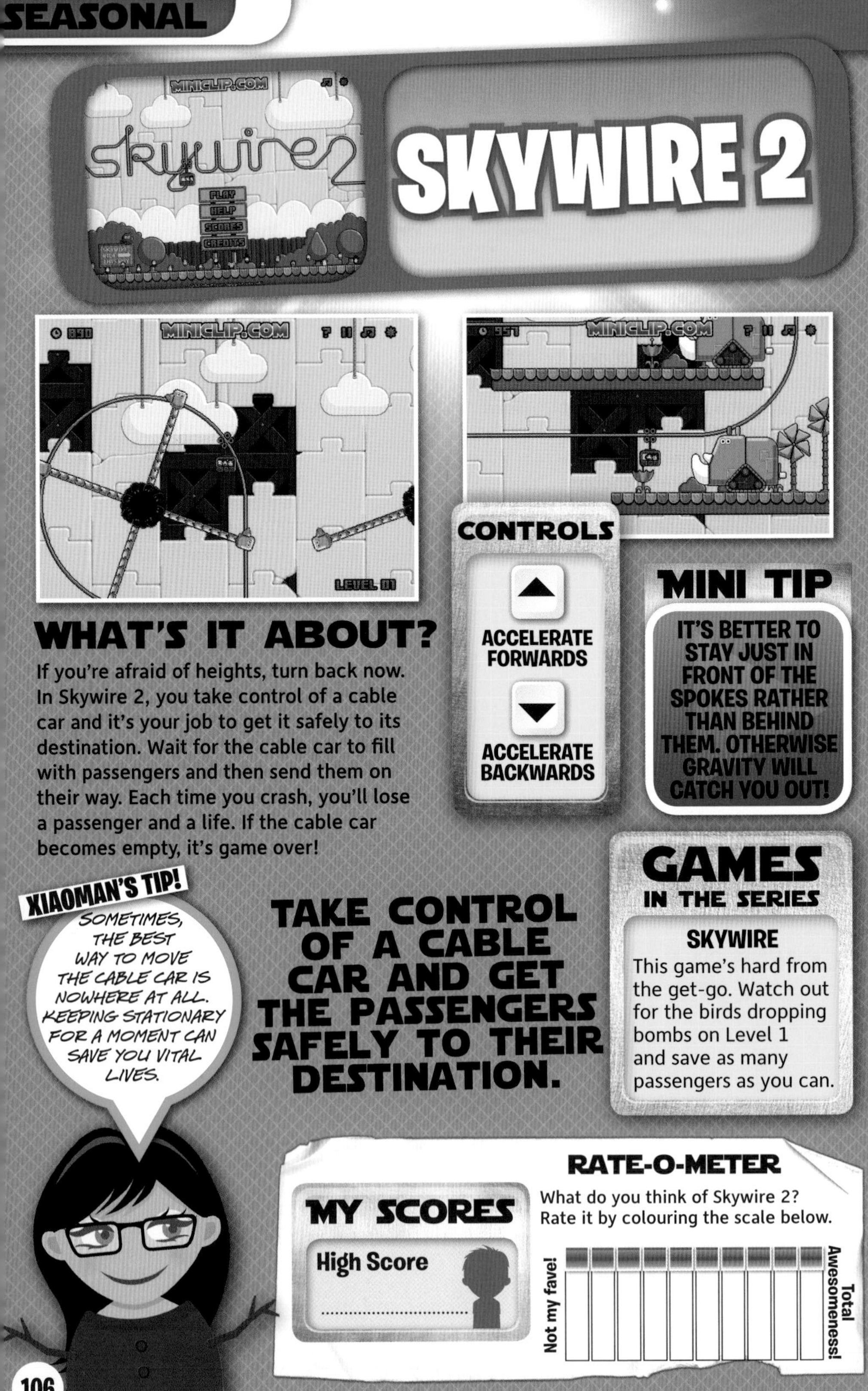

SKYWIRE 2

WHAT'S IT ABOUT?

If you're afraid of heights, turn back now. In Skywire 2, you take control of a cable car and it's your job to get it safely to its destination. Wait for the cable car to fill with passengers and then send them on their way. Each time you crash, you'll lose a passenger and a life. If the cable car becomes empty, it's game over!

CONTROLS

▲ ACCELERATE FORWARDS

▼ ACCELERATE BACKWARDS

MINI TIP

IT'S BETTER TO STAY JUST IN FRONT OF THE SPOKES RATHER THAN BEHIND THEM. OTHERWISE GRAVITY WILL CATCH YOU OUT!

XIAOMAN'S TIP!

SOMETIMES, THE BEST WAY TO MOVE THE CABLE CAR IS NOWHERE AT ALL. KEEPING STATIONARY FOR A MOMENT CAN SAVE YOU VITAL LIVES.

TAKE CONTROL OF A CABLE CAR AND GET THE PASSENGERS SAFELY TO THEIR DESTINATION.

GAMES IN THE SERIES

SKYWIRE

This game's hard from the get-go. Watch out for the birds dropping bombs on Level 1 and save as many passengers as you can.

MY SCORES

High Score ....

RATE-O-METER

What do you think of Skywire 2? Rate it by colouring the scale below.

Not my fave! — Total Awesomeness!

WHAT'S IT ABOUT?

Monster Island is a place where no humans have ever ventured. There, wild creatures battle for ultimate supremacy of the island. Become a monster, use the weapons (known as minis) and aim to become the monster to rule all others. These crazy creatures might look funny, but you won't see them laughing when they explode! Ouch!

CONTROLS

HOLD DOWN, AIM AND RELEASE TO SHOOT

SPACE

CANCEL A THROW

MINI TIP

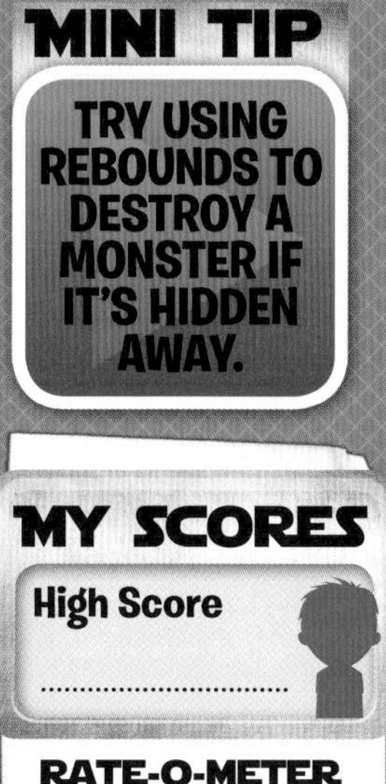

SERGIO'S TIP!

USE EVERYTHING AT YOUR DISPOSAL. REMEMBER, YOU CAN STRIKE BOULDERS AND ROCKS TO KILL OFF THE MONSTERS, TOO.

MY SCORES

High Score

....

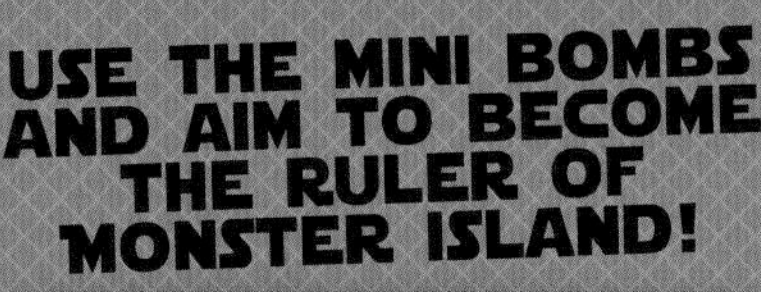

RATE-O-METER

What do you think of Monster Island? Rate it by colouring the scale below.

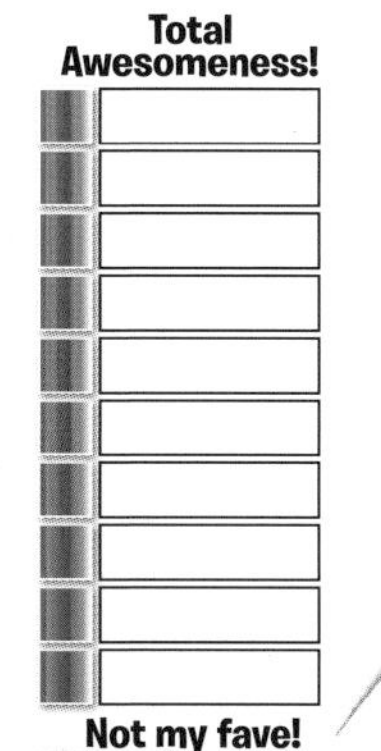

AWARDS

MONSTERS GOLD AWARD
Score **1,400,000** points.

MONSTER NIGHTMARE
Kill 50 monsters and this award is yours!

MONSTER CONQUEROR
Complete all levels to become the ultimate conqueror.

SNOWBALL

WHAT'S IT ABOUT?

It's fun, it's fast, it's snowball pinball! This is unlike any pinball game you have ever seen. Blast the snowballs into the arctic conditions and use the flippers to score as many points as you can. There are so many points up for grabs that this game is seriously addictive. Release the snowballs and go for it!

COME ON PINBALL WIZARDS ... CHARGE THAT SPRING!

SCORE: 20140
SNOWBALLS: 1

ROB'S TIP!

WHEN YOU RELEASE THE SNOWBALL FROM THE SPRING, IT DOESN'T HAVE TO BE POWERFUL. USE THE SPRING WISELY.

CONTROLS

CHARGE SPRING

FLIPPERS

SPACE

MAGNET

MINI TIP

FOR MAXIMUM IMPACT, TRY TO FLICK THE FLIPPERS WHEN THE SNOWBALL IS RIGHT AT THE TIP.

MY SCORES

High Score ....

RATE-O-METER

What do you think of Snowball? Rate it by colouring the scale below.

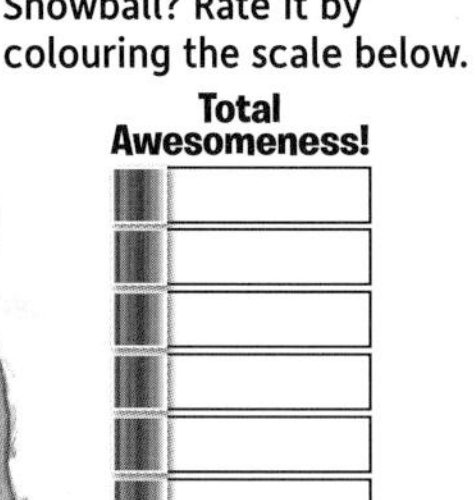

Total Awesomeness!

Not my fave!

AWARDS

GOLD
Collect enough crystals and score **100,000**.

SILVER
You start out with 3 balls, make them count and collect **50,000 points**.

BRONZE
There's snow everywhere. Use it wisely and score **25,000**.

RAFT WARS

WHAT'S IT ABOUT?

Wow! 3-year-old Simon had always dreamt of digging up buried treasure on a beach near his home, and now that's exactly what he's done. He has discovered a bundle of diamonds and gold worth $10 million. But, there's a problem ... pirates, Vikings and more bad guys on the horizon want to grab the treasure. Help Simon and his brother defend their discovery.

ROB'S TIP!

DRAG THE MOUSE FURTHER TO THE RIGHT TO ADD EXTRA FIREPOWER.

SIMON HAS DUG UP BURIED TREASURE. DEFEND IT FROM THE BAD GUYS!

MINI TIP

WATCH OUT FOR THE WATER CREATURES, THEY CAN DEFLECT YOUR SHOTS.

CONTROLS

AIM

FIRE

RATE-O-METER

What do you think of Raft Wars? Rate it by colouring the scale below.

Not my fave! — Total Awesomeness!

MY SCORES

High Score ....

DOODLE 2

WHAT'S IT ABOUT?

Bring the doodle man to life and battle the enemy ... in this case, nasty doodles like eyeballs and monsters! They're there to wipe him out! Use the platform to move vertically and run along the doodle lines. Use your sword to literally erase the enemy, get to the exit and pass the level.

MINI TIP

SOMETIMES, IT'S NOT ABOUT FIGHTING THE ENEMY, BUT TIMING YOUR RUNS TO AVOID THEM.

USE YOUR SWORD TO LITERALLY ERASE THE ENEMY!

MY SCORES

High Score

....

RATE-O-METER

What do you think of Doodle 2? Rate it by colouring the scale below.

Total Awesomeness!

Not my fave!

ROB'S TIP!

AS WELL AS MONSTER ENEMIES, THERE ARE NATURAL ONES TOO. WATCH OUT FOR THE FIRE AND LIGHTNING.

CONTROLS

- ◀ ▶ WALK
- ▲ JUMP
- SPACE FIGHT
- ▼ DUCK

GAMES IN THE SERIES

DOODLE

Is the pencil mightier than the sword? Battle the enemy in this original Doodle game.

BIG JUMP CHALLENGE

WHAT'S IT ABOUT?

Clip on your skis and get to the slopes. Pull off some of the biggest jumps known to man and grab as much air as you can. Now comes the tricky part ... hit those tricks like never before and land safely. Think you've done pretty well? Check out the scores and see how you rate!

ROB'S TIP!

YOU GET FIVE JUMPS, SO TRY TO IMPROVE WITH EACH ONE.

CONTROLS

SPACE – PUSH OFF

▲ ◀ ▼ ▶ – SPIN IN THE AIR

SPACE – GRAB IN THE AIR

PULL OFF THE BIGGEST JUMPS KNOWN TO MAN AND GRAB SOME AIR!

MY SCORES

High Score ....

RATE-O-METER

What do you think of Big Jump Challenge? Rate it by colouring the scale below.

Total Awesomeness!

Not my fave!

MINI TIP

TRICKS ARE ALL WELL AND GOOD, BUT IF YOU DON'T LAND BACK ON YOUR SKIS, IT'S ALL FOR NOTHING.

YOUR INTERACTIVE HUB

Shhhh! The contents of these pages are top secret. The following information gives you access to an amazing online hub that only Miniclip super-fans, that own this handbook, will have. Let's take a look at how to unlock this hidden world.

ACCESSING THE EXCLUSIVE CONTENT

STEP 1

go to: http://www.miniclip.com/insider

STEP 2

Drag Commando from the bottom left of the page to his ammunition in the top right.

UNLOCK SECRET ONLINE CONTENT
STEP 3
Now, just follow the instructions on the screen!
MINICLIP
PLAY GAMES
Live Tournaments!
Play Now!
Signup Login
Action
Sports
Puzzle
Multiplayer
iPhone
Stunt
3D
Motorsports
Sketch Star
RUBBLE TROUBLE MOSCOW
AWARDS
GAMES
CONTROLS
THESE CRAZY GUYS JUST NEVER STOP BLOWING THINGS UP!
ORDER IT NOW!
Hide
Full Categories List
TEST OUR UPCOMING GAMES
Congratulations! You are now a Miniclip games tester. We are relying on you for feedback on the most recently developed games to make sure they are perfect.
EXCLUSIVE GAME PREVIEWS
Get a load of this! The Miniclip team will give you the chance to check out the latest games before anyone else gets a chance. You've gotta love that!
WIN GOODIES!
Now that you are a Miniclip VIP, you get the chance to win stacks of awesome stuff online!
113

ALEXANDER

PAGE 116

FAVE MOTORSPORT GAME:
MONSTER TRUCKS NITRO 2

WHY? Big trucks that crush anything in their path has to be a good thing!

HIGH SCORE
GOLDS ON EVERY LEVEL AND JUMPED 20.4M IN THE HIGH FLYER LEVEL & 50.3M IN THE LONG JUMP LEVEL

JANE

PAGE 120

FAVE MOTORSPORT GAME:
MOTOCROSS COUNTRY FEVER

WHY? This multiplayer motocross game really brings out my competitive side.

HIGH SCORE
176,200

NICLAS

PAGE 118

FAVE MOTORSPORT GAME:
SUPERBIKE RACE OFF

WHY? Gives me the perfect chance to be a speed demon!

HIGH SCORE
01:31:28

ZAINA

PAGE 124

FAVE MOTORSPORT GAME:
TURBO RACING 2

WHY? Burning rubber through these streets is massive fun, especially when you get to move up through the ranks.

HIGH SCORE
61,800

MOTORSPORT GAMES

If it has an engine, you'll find it here! This chapter is packed with ten of the fastest, noisiest racing games on the planet. Planes, quad bikes, monster trucks and futuristic cars all feature here. So, choose your wheels and burn some rubber!

MONSTER TRUCKS NITRO 2

WHAT'S IT ABOUT?

These monster trucks are serious destroyers! Select your truck, receive your mission and drive your massive vehicle over jumps, trains and airplanes. Hit the accelerator and crush everything in your path. You're racing against the clock so don't stop, just power on through.

THESE MONSTER TRUCKS ARE SERIOUS DESTROYERS!

ALEXANDER'S TIP!

THIS GAME IS MORE ABOUT BALANCE THAN SPEED. WATCH THAT YOU DON'T TILT BACKWARDS OR FORWARDS TOO MUCH.

CRUSH AND DESTROY EVERYTHING IN YOUR PATH!
MY SCORES
High Score
RATE-O-METER
What do you think of Monster Trucks Nitro 2? Rate it by colouring the scale below.
Total Awesomeness!
Not my fave!
MINI TIP
COLLECT NITRO BOOSTS FOR EXTRA POWER!
CONTROLS
DRIVE YOUR MONSTER TRUCK
GAMES IN THE SERIES
MONSTER TRUCKS
Crush cars and perform incredible stunts, plus check out the awesome wheel spikes!
MONSTER TRUCKS NITRO
Drive over some of the best tracks around. Watch out for the rolling logs!
TIME 00:13
MINICLIP RedLynx
00:08
MINICLIP RedLynx
MINICLIP
Mission: Time trial
Time left: 00:29

SUPERBIKE RACE OFF™

WHAT'S IT ABOUT?

Calling all bikers! Jump onto the seat of some of the fastest bikes around and take to the track. This is a 3D racing game that will blast you into the stratosphere with the sheer speed and agility of the game play. As you advance through the levels you can even head to the garage to upgrade your bike. Now, head to the starting line and let your engine roar!

MINI TIP

DON'T OVERSTEER OR YOU'LL BE IN BIG TROUBLE!

CONTROLS

▲ ◀ ▼ ▶
RIDE

▲
DOUBLE TAP FOR TURBO

S
SOUND

P
PAUSE

NICLAS' TIP!

CHECK OUT THE REAL-TIME RACING OPTION AGAINST YOUR FRIENDS ON FACEBOOK!

HEAD TO THE STARTING LINE AND LET YOUR ENGINE ROAR IN THIS AWESOME 3D GAME!

MY SCORES

High Score

....

RATE-O-METER

What do you think of Superbike Race Off? Rate it by colouring the scale below.

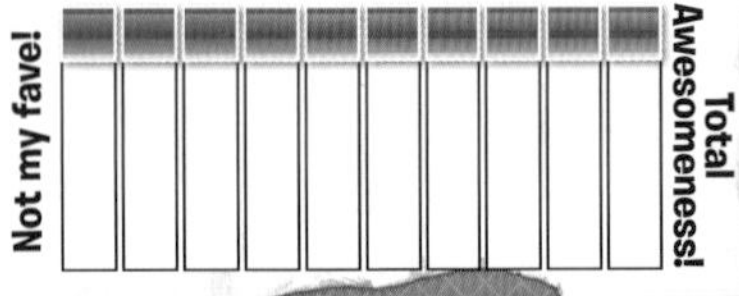

AGENT: FREERIDE AQUA ESCAPE™

WHAT'S IT ABOUT?

Agent Freeride returns, and this time he has a licence to escape! The mission is set and the pressure is on. Agent Freeride had stolen some top-secret documents, outlining the plans for a weapon-equipped water bike. Help him escape from the organisation's henchmen in this super-charged, action-packed game!

CONTROLS

▲ ▼ ACCELERATE AND REVERSE

◀ ▶ STEER

Z USE GADGET

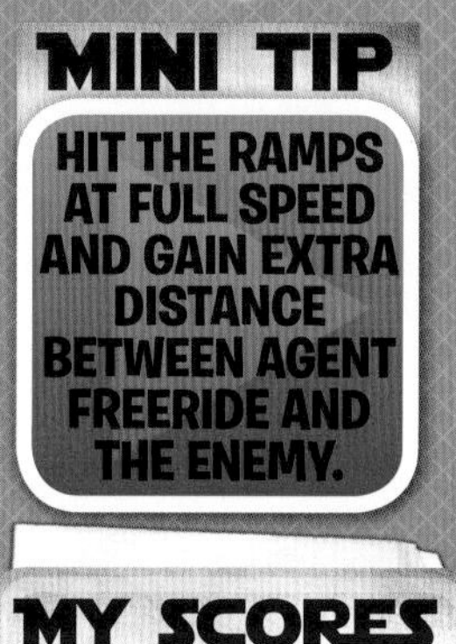

MINI TIP

HIT THE RAMPS AT FULL SPEED AND GAIN EXTRA DISTANCE BETWEEN AGENT FREERIDE AND THE ENEMY.

MY SCORES

High Score

....

RATE-O-METER

What do you think of Agent: Freeride Aqua Escape? Rate it by colouring the scale below.

Total Awesomeness!

Not my fave!

IT'S TIME TO GET WET IN THIS AWESOME AGENT ADVENTURE GAME!

ROB'S TIP!

WATCH OUT FOR THE MINES. HIT THOSE AND YOUR ENERGY LEVEL WILL DROP PRETTY QUICKLY!

AWARDS

GOLD
For this golden award you need **125,000 points**.

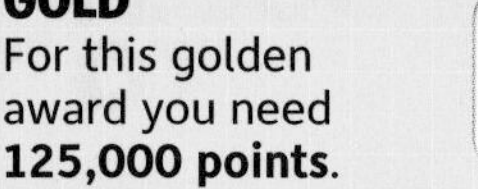

SILVER
Use your gadgets to help get a score of **75,000 points**.

BRONZE
Escape from the enemy base and score **30,000 points**.

MOTOCROSS COUNTRY FEVER

WHAT'S IT ABOUT?

It's 3D motocross with a country twist! Ride that dirt bike across the torn-up countryside tracks in a three-way chase. Boost your score to the max by smashing through any objects that lay in your way and race to the finish against some of the toughest competition around. It's as awesome as two-wheel racing gets!

CONTROLS

DRIVE

AWARDS

Gold
Tear up these tough country tracks and score **100,000 points**.

Silver
Make motocross madness and score **85,000 points**.

Bronze
Maneuver that dirt bike and score **70,000 points**.

SMASH THOUGH EVERYTHING AND BOOST YOUR SCORE TO THE MAX!

JANE'S TIP!

KEEP CHECKING OUT THE CIRCUIT MAP ON THE LEFT TO SEE HOW YOU'RE FARING AGAINST YOUR COMPETITORS.

3D MOTOCROSS WITH A COUNTRY TWIST!

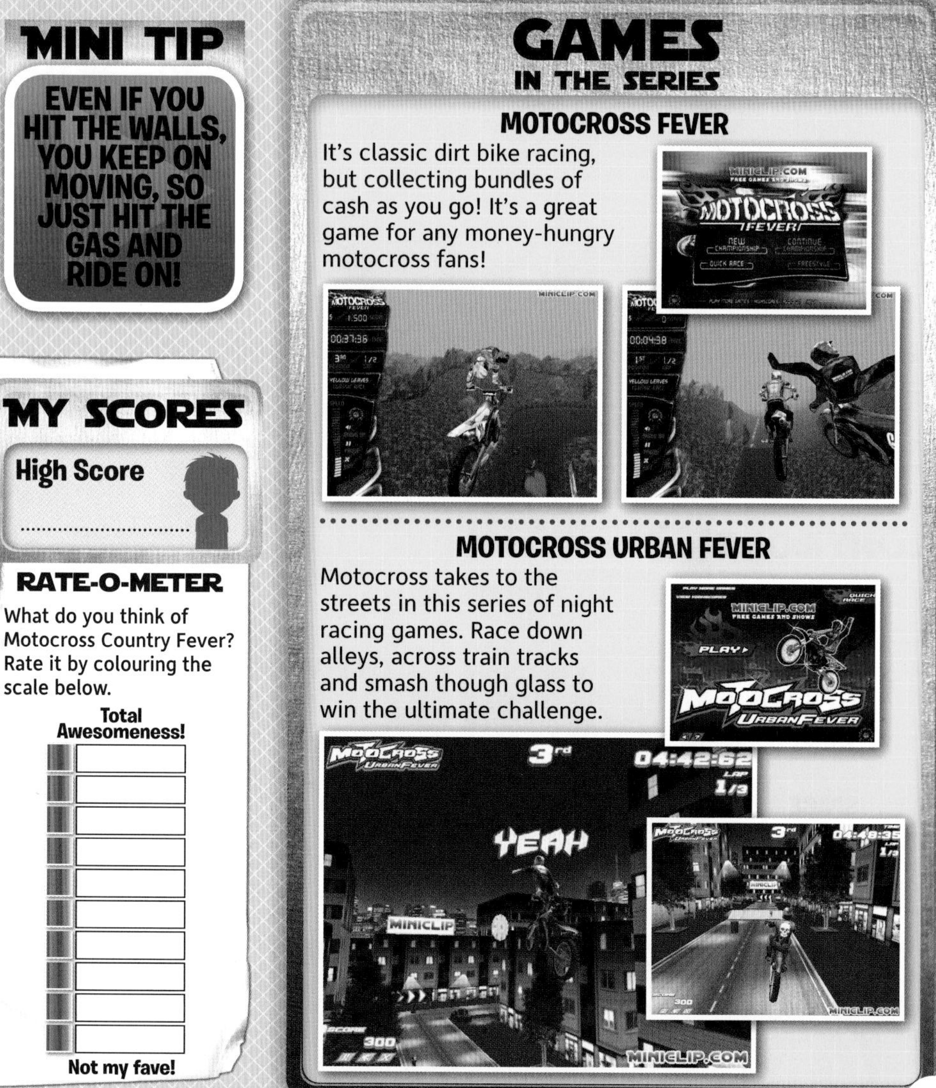

MINI TIP

EVEN IF YOU HIT THE WALLS, YOU KEEP ON MOVING, SO JUST HIT THE GAS AND RIDE ON!

MY SCORES

High Score

....

RATE-O-METER

What do you think of Motocross Country Fever? Rate it by colouring the scale below.

Total Awesomeness!

Not my fave!

GAMES IN THE SERIES

MOTOCROSS FEVER

It's classic dirt bike racing, but collecting bundles of cash as you go! It's a great game for any money-hungry motocross fans!

MOTOCROSS URBAN FEVER

Motocross takes to the streets in this series of night racing games. Race down alleys, across train tracks and smash though glass to win the ultimate challenge.

FORMULA RACING

WHAT'S IT ABOUT?

The race is on! In Quick Race mode, head to the pit to pick your car, choose the circuit and get ready to roar down the track. If you're up for a greater challenge, then hit tournament mode, add your racing name and prepare for some pretty tough competition. Look out for the chances to go turbo and mind you don't crash too many times. If you wreck your car, you'll be out of the race.

RATE-O-METER

What do you think of Formula Racing? Rate it by colouring the scale below.

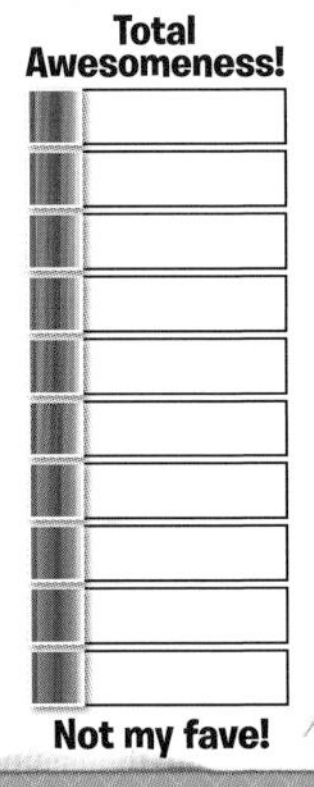

MINI TIP

IT'S ALL TO PLAY FOR AT THE START. TRY TO SWERVE IN FRONT OF THE OTHER CARS AS QUICKLY AS YOU CAN.

THE RACE IS ON! HEAD TO THE PIT AND PREPARE TO ROAR DOWN THE TRACK.

KEEP AN EYE ON THE DAMAGE LEVEL IN THE BOTTOM RIGHT CORNER. YOU CAN REPAIR YOUR VEHICLE BY DRIVING THROUGH THE SPANNER ICONS.

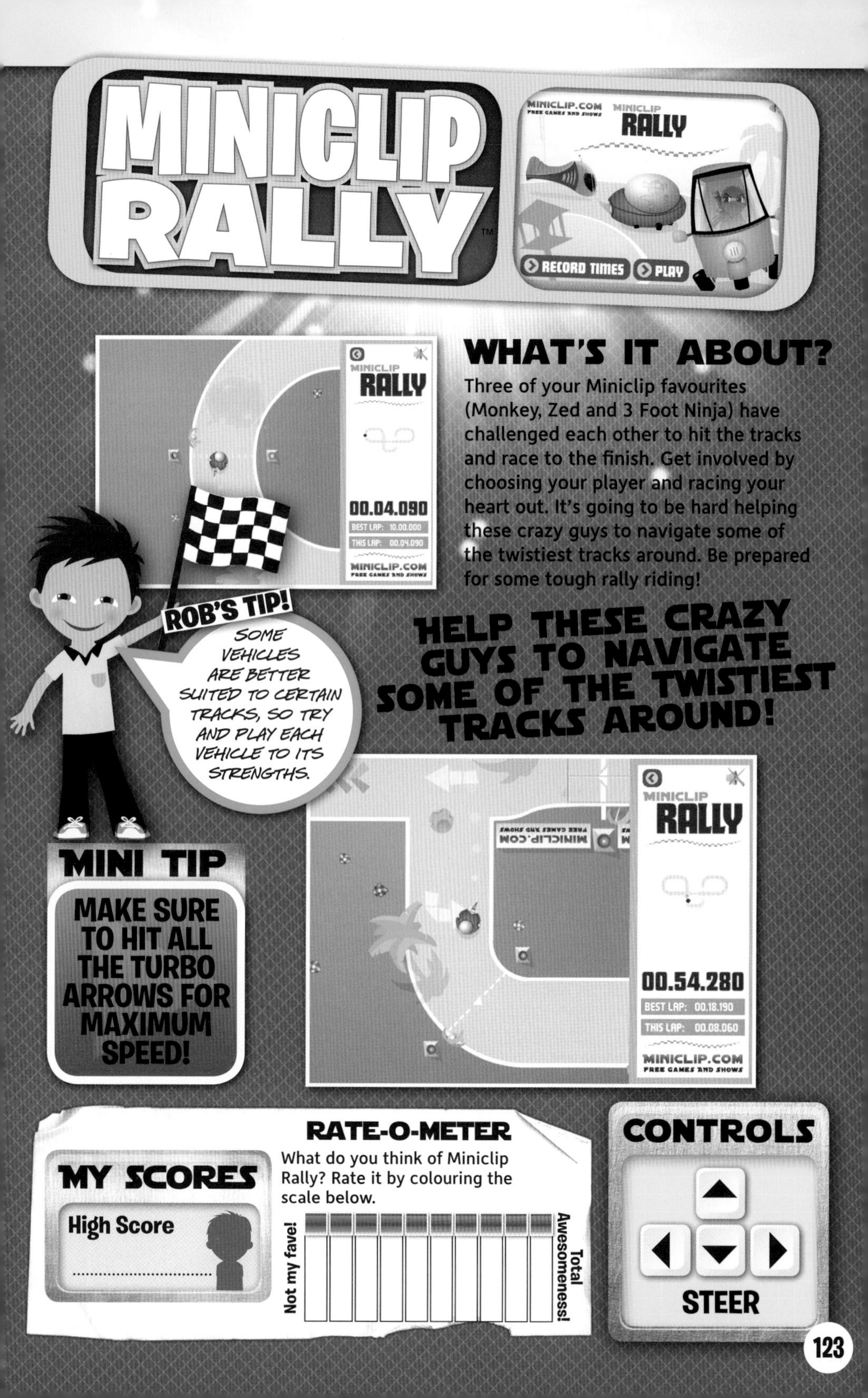

MINICLIP RALLY™

WHAT'S IT ABOUT?

Three of your Miniclip favourites (Monkey, Zed and 3 Foot Ninja) have challenged each other to hit the tracks and race to the finish. Get involved by choosing your player and racing your heart out. It's going to be hard helping these crazy guys to navigate some of the twistiest tracks around. Be prepared for some tough rally riding!

HELP THESE CRAZY GUYS TO NAVIGATE SOME OF THE TWISTIEST TRACKS AROUND!

MINI TIP

MAKE SURE TO HIT ALL THE TURBO ARROWS FOR MAXIMUM SPEED!

MY SCORES

High Score

....

RATE-O-METER

What do you think of Miniclip Rally? Rate it by colouring the scale below.

Not my fave!

Total Awesomeness!

CONTROLS

STEER

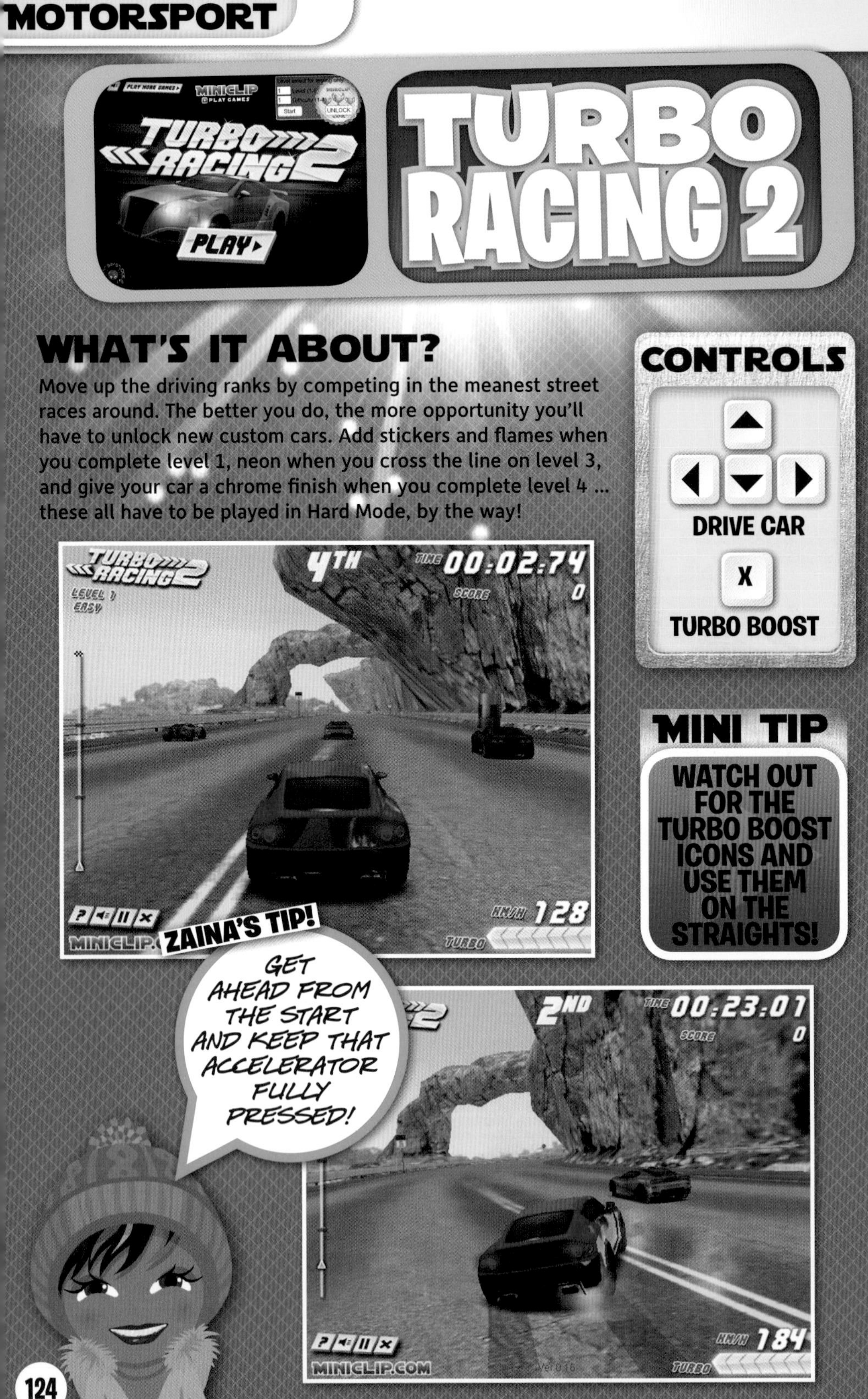

TURBO RACING 2

WHAT'S IT ABOUT?

Move up the driving ranks by competing in the meanest street races around. The better you do, the more opportunity you'll have to unlock new custom cars. Add stickers and flames when you complete level 1, neon when you cross the line on level 3, and give your car a chrome finish when you complete level 4 ... these all have to be played in Hard Mode, by the way!

CONTROLS

▲ ◀ ▼ ▶ DRIVE CAR

X TURBO BOOST

MINI TIP

WATCH OUT FOR THE TURBO BOOST ICONS AND USE THEM ON THE STRAIGHTS!

ZAINA'S TIP!

GET AHEAD FROM THE START AND KEEP THAT ACCELERATOR FULLY PRESSED!

HEAD TO THE STARTING LINE, REV IT UP AND GET RACING!

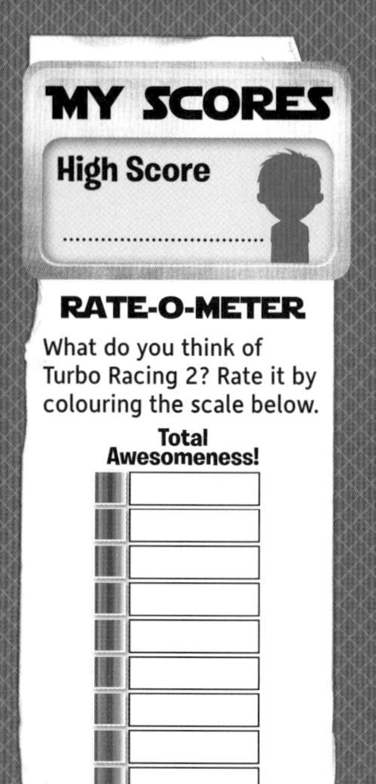

MY SCORES

High Score

....

RATE-O-METER

What do you think of Turbo Racing 2? Rate it by colouring the scale below.

Total Awesomeness!

Not my fave!

GAMES IN THE SERIES

TURBO RACING

It's a race to the finish. The last car on each lap is eliminated, so keep your pedal to the metal!

DEVELOPER Q&A

Name: Oslo Albet Roig
Age: 24
Lives: Barcelona, Spain

How did you get started in game development?

I started out doing some Flash animations for a web page, nothing fancy. Then, when I started my degree in Mathematics, they taught me how to program. It was then that I decided I wanted to create Flash games. I taught myself AS3 coding via some links on the Internet, and I made my first game called 'Towers' in 2006. It was a big moment for me!

Do you make a lot of money doing it?

I can't complain! This is my first year since leaving university and I made the decision to work on my games full-time. Luckily, the 'FireBoy & WaterGirl' series has been really successful, so I can pretty much live off the ad revenue from these games!

What's your favourite game on Miniclip (not made by you)?

Bloxorz, without any doubt. It has the perfect combination of difficulty and simplicity!

What advice would you give someone who wanted to work in games?

Tutorials, tutorials, tutorials! There's lots of free tutorials on the internet that can teach you everything you need to know. Start with simple apps and, in time, you will have the knowledge and experience to produce a great game.

Name: Sebastian Barabanow
Age: 35
Lives: Szczecin, Poland

What's the hardest thing about game development?

I'd say the logistics. A good game brings three elements together: great performing code, awesome graphics and excellent gameplay (the hardest thing of all). You need to find super-talented people in each of these fields and arrange a situation where they can be creative under the limitations of time and budget.

What game are you most proud of?

There are many games I'm proud of, but one that I value for the great time I had working on it is Mister Easter. It is a small game, but the team developed it in one huge creative leap, just before the Easter holidays. It was tons of fun! Check it out on Miniclip.

Where do you get your ideas for games?

We are all dedicated gamers, so usually ideas come when we play games we love. We just sit and thinking how awesome a game is, how well it is built, when suddenly a wild idea will appear and you just can't shake it.

How many people in your team? What do they do?

We have over 60 people on board. The majority of the team are developers and artists who basically do all the heavy work.

What's your favourite game of all time?

I'm an old-school guy, raised on classic adventure games, so there can be only one – The Secret Of Monkey Island! You guys should all check it out – it's a classic!

BRYONY

PAGE 136

FAVE SHOOT 'EM UP & TOWER DEFENSE GAME:
COMMANDO 3

WHY?: The fact that I can single-handedly prevent World War III makes this shoot 'em up game very cool indeed!

HIGH SCORE
2,644,350

GLEN

PAGE 139

FAVE SHOOT 'EM UP & TOWER DEFENSE GAME:
CANYON DEFENSE

WHY? To have the odds stacked against you and still come out on top when you are fighting the ultimate enemy feels good!

HIGH SCORE
197,694

JAMIE

PAGE 138

FAVE SHOOT 'EM UP & TOWER DEFENSE GAME:
ZOMBIE DEFENSE AGENCY

WHY? I could build barricades and slay zombies all day long ... that is all!

HIGH SCORE
1,523,450

NICLAS

PAGE 132

FAVE SHOOT 'EM UP & TOWER DEFENSE GAME:
ROBO RAMPAGE

WHY? Mega metal crunching machines from the future make me smile a lot!

HIGH SCORE
2,584

SHOOT 'EM UP AND TOWER DEFENSE GAMES

Whether you're taking out an opponent or defending your village against an onslaught, your ultimate task is to come out on top. These games are solely for winners, who are willing to battle until the end and gain a victory ... no matter the cost!

CHECK OUT A STACK OF WICKED SHOOT 'EM UP AND TOWER DEFENSE GAMES

HAMBO

WHAT'S IT ABOUT?

Hambo is on a mission to bring home the Bacon ... literally! His friend, Bacon, has been kidnapped and its up to you to help this porky hero rescue him. Armed only with his crossbow, a series of super-charged ammo and his cunning wiles, this battle-hungry pig means serious business. Take aim, fire and explode those piggy enemies ... and don't get killed in action!

CONTROLS

HOLD DOWN, AIM AND RELEASE TO SHOOT

MINI TIP

GRENADES HAVE A 3-SECOND FUSE, SO MAKE SURE THEY LAND WHERE THEY CAN HAVE TIME TO DETONATE.

THIS BATTLE-HUNGRY PIG MEANS SERIOUS COMBAT BUSINESS!

MINI TIP

TRY TO COMPLETE EACH LEVEL AS BEST YOU CAN TO ACHIEVE A GOLD STANDARD MEDAL.

MY SCORES

High Score

....

RATE-O-METER

What do you think of Hambo? Rate it by colouring the scale below.

Total Awesomeness!

Not my fave!

HAMBO IS ON A MISSION TO BRING HOME THE BACON!

ROBO RAMPAGE

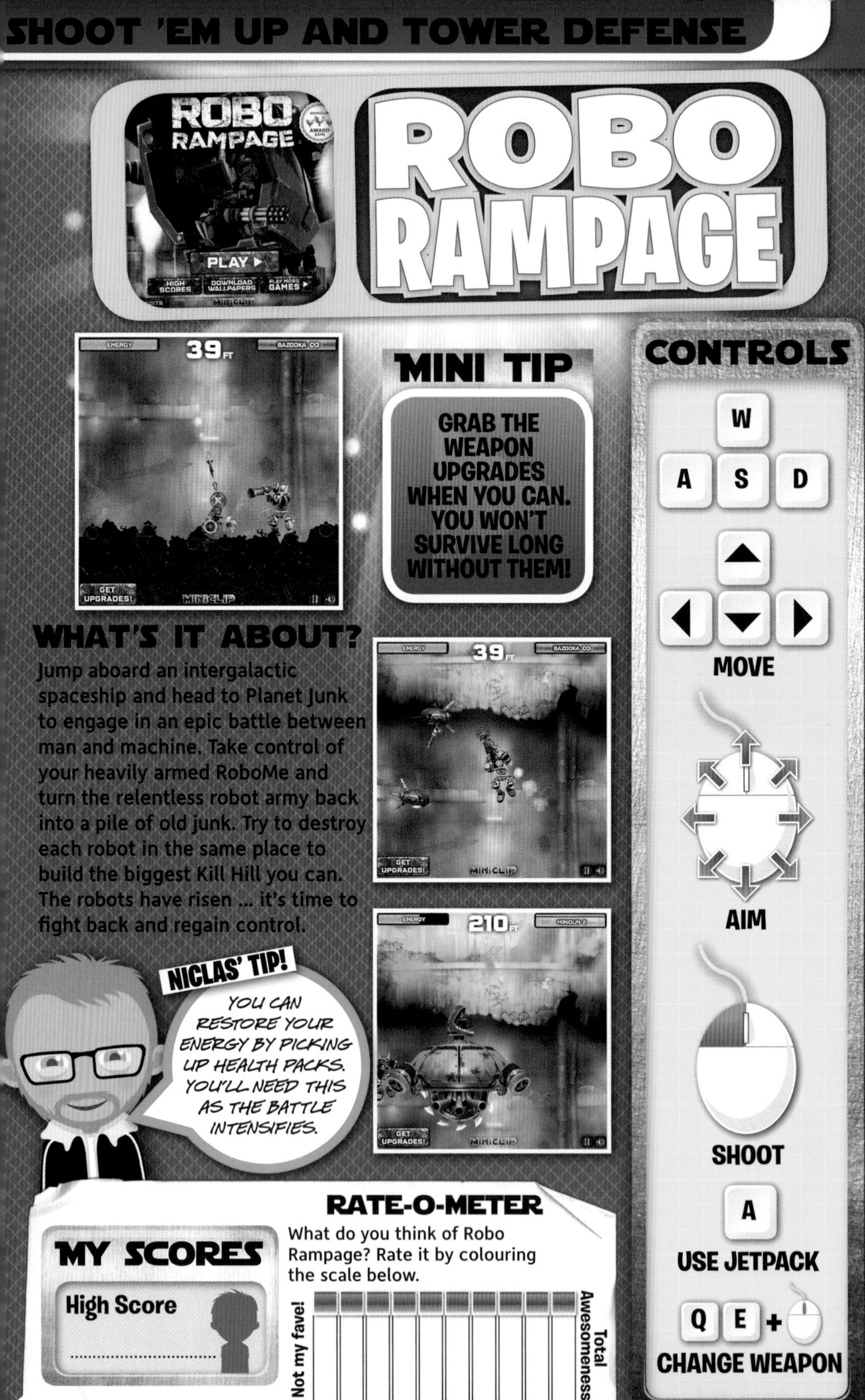

MINI TIP

GRAB THE WEAPON UPGRADES WHEN YOU CAN. YOU WON'T SURVIVE LONG WITHOUT THEM!

CONTROLS

W A S D / arrow keys — MOVE

Mouse — AIM

Mouse click — SHOOT

A — USE JETPACK

Q E + mouse — CHANGE WEAPON

WHAT'S IT ABOUT?

Jump aboard an intergalactic spaceship and head to Planet Junk to engage in an epic battle between man and machine. Take control of your heavily armed RoboMe and turn the relentless robot army back into a pile of old junk. Try to destroy each robot in the same place to build the biggest Kill Hill you can. The robots have risen ... it's time to fight back and regain control.

RATE-O-METER

What do you think of Robo Rampage? Rate it by colouring the scale below.

Not my fave! — Total Awesomeness!

MY SCORES

High Score

....

FIGHTER PILOT 2

WHAT'S IT ABOUT?

Take to the air in this vintage fighter pilot game. Become the ultimate airborne hero and engage in air-to-air combat to end the Great War. Take the controls and out-maneouvre the enemy to evade the onslaught of bullets. You'll be handed a mission at the beginning of each level and need to complete the tasks to move to the next stage. Good luck, fighter ace!

CONTROLS

▲ ◀ ▼ ▶
FLY

SPACE
SHOOT

A
DROP BOMBS

MINI TIP

TRY TO COMPLETE THE 'TIPS' THAT ARE HANDED OUT WHEN THE MISSION STARTS. YOU'LL GAIN EXTRA POINTS.

ROB'S TIP!

BECOME A PRO AT THE 360-DEGREE LOOP TO OUTSMART THE ENEMY.

MY SCORES

High Score

....

RATE-O-METER

What do you think of Fighter Pilot 2? Rate it by colouring the scale below.

Total Awesomeness!

Not my fave!

GAMES IN THE SERIES

FIGHTER PILOT
Not only are you taking down the air enemy, but you need to destroy the ground forces, too!

AWARDS

Gold
Score **50,000 points** to become a legend of the skies.

Silver
Shoot down anything the enemy can throw at you and gain **30,000 points**.

Bronze
Prove yourself a worthy pilot and score **15,000 points**.

CANYON SHOOTER 2

WHAT'S IT ABOUT?

Choose your character and then leap into the void of this futuristic canyon to take on the enemy. Aim with precision and destroy as many bad guys as you can on your descent. It's dangerous and windy up there, so be prepared for a rough ride. When the time comes, land on a building and fight your foes on solid ground.

MINI TIP

THE ENEMY MOVE AROUND A LOT IN THE AIR. FOCUS ON KEEPING THEM IN YOUR TARGET.

CONTROLS

GAMES IN THE SERIES

CANYON SHOOTER
Parachutes at the ready! It's time to take to the sky and target the enemy in this original canyon game.

AWARDS

Gold
Defeat all the bosses, use all the ammo and get amazing combos to score **600,000 points**!

Silver
Chain together great combos and shoot down anything you see to score **500,000 points**.

Bronze
Score **300,000 points** to win the bronze!

THE CANYON'S DANGEROUS AND WINDY, SO BE PREPARED FOR A ROUGH RIDE!

MY SCORES

High Score

RATE-O-METER

What do you think of Canyon Shooter 2? Rate it by colouring the scale below.

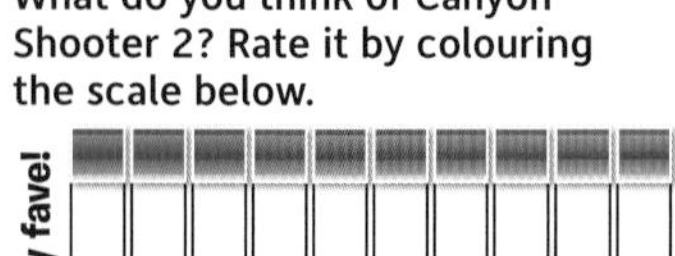

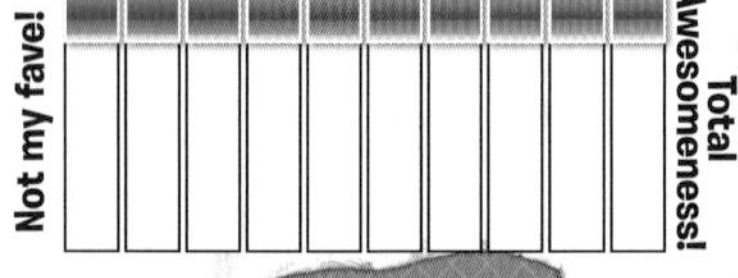

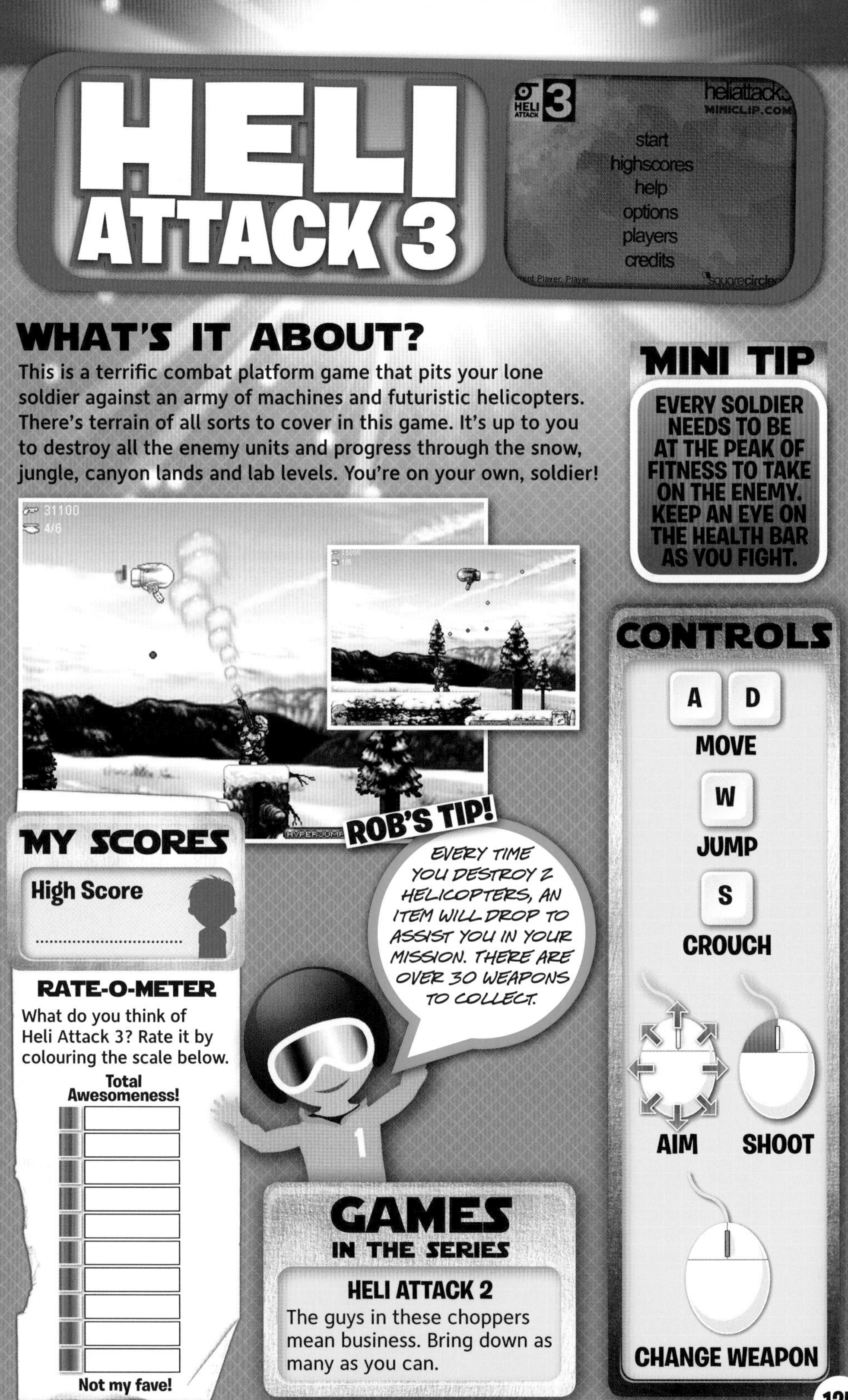

HELI ATTACK 3

WHAT'S IT ABOUT?

This is a terrific combat platform game that pits your lone soldier against an army of machines and futuristic helicopters. There's terrain of all sorts to cover in this game. It's up to you to destroy all the enemy units and progress through the snow, jungle, canyon lands and lab levels. You're on your own, soldier!

MINI TIP

EVERY SOLDIER NEEDS TO BE AT THE PEAK OF FITNESS TO TAKE ON THE ENEMY. KEEP AN EYE ON THE HEALTH BAR AS YOU FIGHT.

ROB'S TIP!

EVERY TIME YOU DESTROY 2 HELICOPTERS, AN ITEM WILL DROP TO ASSIST YOU IN YOUR MISSION. THERE ARE OVER 30 WEAPONS TO COLLECT.

CONTROLS

A D — MOVE

W — JUMP

S — CROUCH

AIM — SHOOT

CHANGE WEAPON

MY SCORES

High Score

....

RATE-O-METER

What do you think of Heli Attack 3? Rate it by colouring the scale below.

Total Awesomeness!

Not my fave!

GAMES IN THE SERIES

HELI ATTACK 2

The guys in these choppers mean business. Bring down as many as you can.

COMMANDO 3™

WHAT'S IT ABOUT?

Hot on the heels of its Commando forerunners, this generation of the game has way more war than before! Take your commando through Russia and Egypt before doing a total 360 and blasting your way back to Europe through Berlin and Normandy. No pressure during this game – it's just the ultimate prevention of World War III is resting entirely on your shoulders! Feelin' the weight yet? Come on Commando ... get to that battlefield!

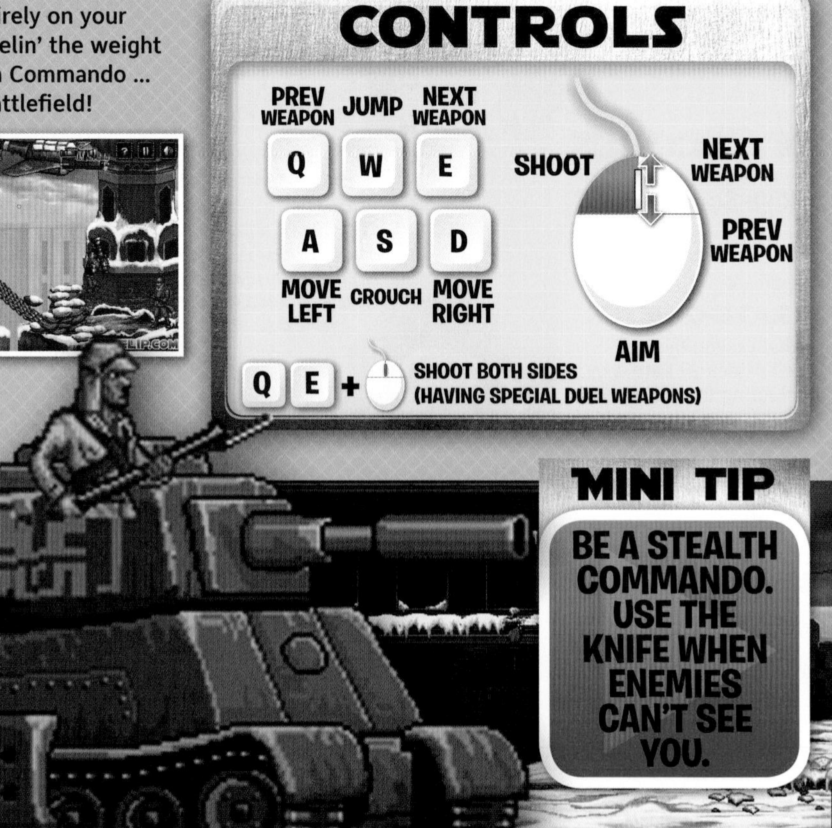

MINI TIP

BE A STEALTH COMMANDO. USE THE KNIFE WHEN ENEMIES CAN'T SEE YOU.

COME ON COMMANDO ... GET TO THAT BATTLEFIELD!

AWARDS

Commando Master
Play the Hard Mode and score a massive **7,000,000 points**.

Gold
Defeat every boss, destroy all the levels and score **3,000,000 points**!

Silver
Use every weapon at your disposal and destroy everything in your path whilst scoring **2,000,000 points**.

Bronze
Simple! Just score **1,000,000 points** to gain this award.

MY SCORES

High Score

....

RATE-O-METER

What do you think of Commando III? Rate it by colouring the scale below.

Total Awesomeness!

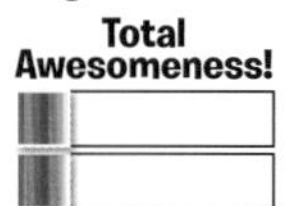

Not my fave!

BRYONY'S TIP!

DON'T CONSTANTLY CHANGE YOUR WEAPONS. YOU MIGHT RUN OUT OF AMMO!

GAMES IN THE SERIES

COMMANDO
This is where the entire saga began, gamers! You need to help defend the allies from the evil scourge of Europe.

COMMANDO II
In this sequel, our hero continues his battle with more missions, more enemies and a bigger artillery.

COMMANDO ASSAULT
We see the brave Commando join forces with his allies to hold off the relentless waves of enemies!

COMMANDO DEFENSE
The enemy is attempting a sneak attack on Commando. Time to fortify your ground and take 'em down!

ZOMBIE DEFENSE AGENCY

WHAT'S IT ABOUT?

It's your worst nightmare as a pack of crazy zombies are about to descend on your town. But things are worse than you imagine ... the zombie population are absolutely starving and they're out to fill their gurgling stomachs! You must join the Zombie Defense Agency and protect the town. Build barricades and destroy the living dead before they gobble you up!

JAMIE'S TIP!

PLACE YOUR WEAPONS WISELY AND LOOK OUT FOR UPGRADES.

MINI TIP

TRY NOT TO LET EVEN A SINGLE ZOMBIE THROUGH THE BARRICADE. IF ONE GETS THROUGH THEN THE FIGHT BECOMES MUCH HARDER!

MY SCORES

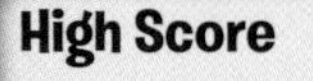

High Score

....

RATE-O-METER

What do you think of Zombie Defense Agency? Rate it by colouring the scale below.

Total Awesomeness!

Not my fave!

CONTROLS

BUILD TOWERS

AWARDS

Gold
Become a Master Tactician of the Agency and score **600,000 points**.

Silver
Build a zombie defense and score **300,000 points**.

Bronze
Fight off the zombies and score **60,000 points**.

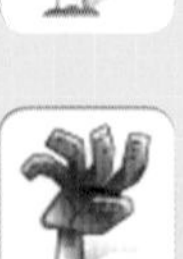

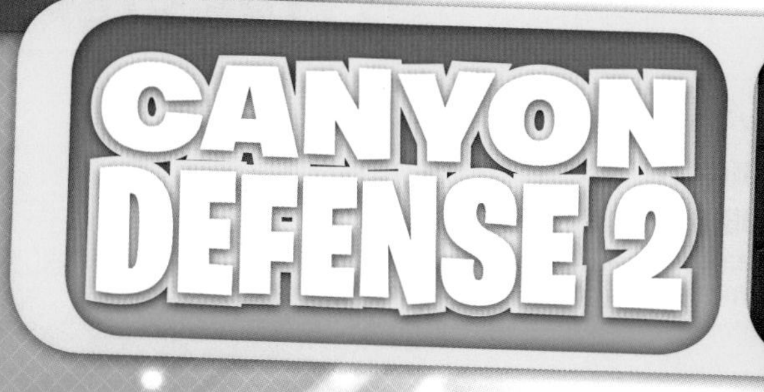

Life was once peaceful in this remote canyon, where the inhabitants lived happily on sacred land. However, nothing will ever be the same again. The ultimate machinery of destruction has descended to wreak havoc on these poor people. You must defend your village and the population with some of the most sophisticated anti-war equipment ever created. Defend the base at all costs and keep the enemy at bay.

DEFEND THE BASE FROM THE ADVANCING ENEMY!

MINI TIP

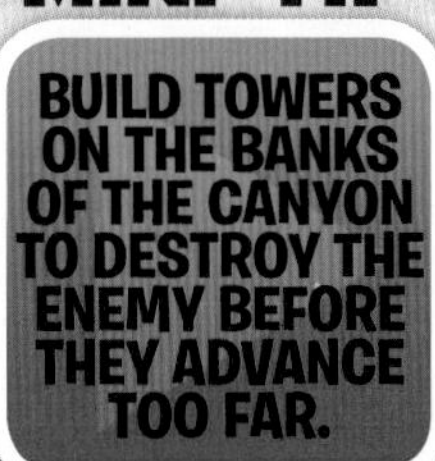

GLENN'S TIP!

LOOK OUT FOR THE UPGRADE TASKS. THESE WILL ALLOW YOU TO HAVE ACCESS TO NEW DEFENSE TOWERS.

THERE ARE 10 AWARDS TO AIM FOR. HERE'S A FEW OF THEM!

AWARDS

Canyon Gold award
Complete all levels with the gold ranking.

Canyon General award
Achieve the rank General to unlock this award.

Canyon Defense 2 Beginner
First things first ... complete level one!

GAMES IN THE SERIES

CANYON DEFENSE
Build a solid defense system and protect the inhabitants of the canyon.

MY SCORES

RATE-O-METER

What do you think of Canyon Defense 2? Rate it by colouring the scale below.

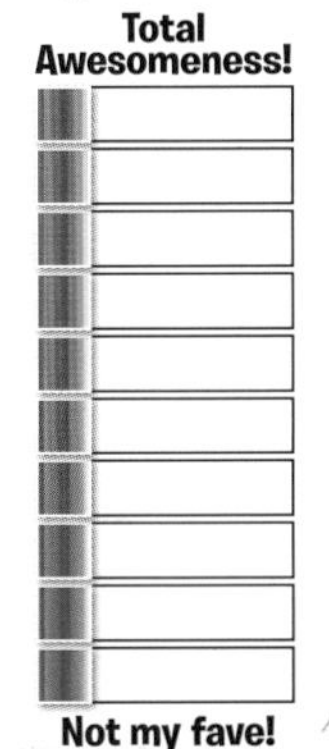

ALEXANDER

JOB TITLE: Head of Games

JOB DESCRIPTION: I work with a great team of people to find the best games to go on Miniclip.com.

BEN

JOB TITLE: Director of Web Development

JOB DESCRIPTION: I help the website team to make amazing stuff - I also like to design pretty web pages.

JAMIE

JOB TITLE: Quality Assurance Games Tester

JOB DESCRIPTION: I make sure the games work the way they should. I play games for a living!

JANE

JOB TITLE: Operation Team Leader

JOB DESCRIPTION: I make sure all awesome games and features are working on our site and keep eye on MC forums as well.

NICLAS

JOB TITLE: Creative Director

JOB DESCRIPTION: I design games and work with fantastic developers and artists to make them happen.

ROB L.

JOB TITLE: Game Development Manager

JOB DESCRIPTION: I find awesome games and work with developers to make good games great.

STAFF FAVES

Everyone has their favourite Miniclip game, but what do the people who work at Miniclip think of the awesome online collection they have created? We asked a few of them for their top games. Check out their choices. Are any of them the same as yours?

ROB

JOB TITLE: CEO / Co-founder

JOB DESCRIPTION: I work with the amazing Miniclip people and partners to make sure our players have the most fun we can give them.

THERESE

JOB TITLE: Quality Assurance Manager

JOB DESCRIPTION: I make sure games are as awesome as they can be before going live.

CHECK OUT THE MINICLIP TEAM'S FAVOURITE GAMES

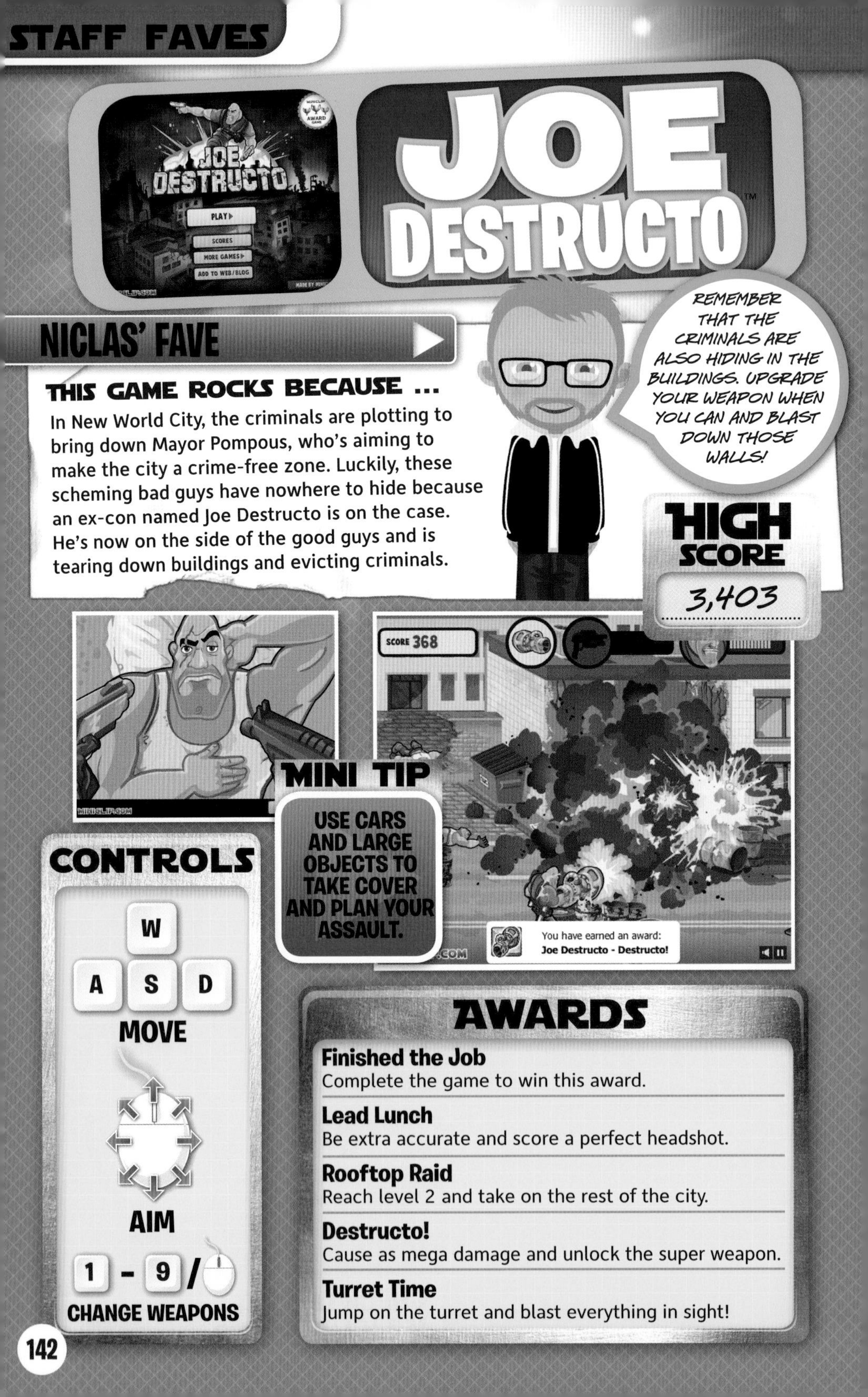

JOE DESTRUCTO™

NICLAS' FAVE

THIS GAME ROCKS BECAUSE ...

In New World City, the criminals are plotting to bring down Mayor Pompous, who's aiming to make the city a crime-free zone. Luckily, these scheming bad guys have nowhere to hide because an ex-con named Joe Destructo is on the case. He's now on the side of the good guys and is tearing down buildings and evicting criminals.

REMEMBER THAT THE CRIMINALS ARE ALSO HIDING IN THE BUILDINGS. UPGRADE YOUR WEAPON WHEN YOU CAN AND BLAST DOWN THOSE WALLS!

HIGH SCORE

3,403

MINI TIP

USE CARS AND LARGE OBJECTS TO TAKE COVER AND PLAN YOUR ASSAULT.

CONTROLS

W A S D — MOVE

AIM

1 - 9 / — CHANGE WEAPONS

AWARDS

Finished the Job
Complete the game to win this award.

Lead Lunch
Be extra accurate and score a perfect headshot.

Rooftop Raid
Reach level 2 and take on the rest of the city.

Destructo!
Cause as mega damage and unlock the super weapon.

Turret Time
Jump on the turret and blast everything in sight!

ZOMBOTRON

ROB'S FAVE

THIS GAME ROCKS BECAUSE ...

Welcome to the planet Zombotron. It's unlike anywhere you've been before. The trouble is, it's populated with evil zombies, and they're out to eat everything in their path! Bio-robots have been created to head to the planet and rid it of these evil beings – you are one of them. Prepare for the mission of a lifetime and good luck!

YOU CAN PRESERVE AMMO BY PUSHING OBJECTS ON TO THE ZOMBIES TO ELIMINATE THEM.

HIGH SCORE

218,637

CONTROLS

- Arrow keys: MOVE
- E: PERFORM ACTION
- Mouse: AIM AND SHOOT
- R: RELOAD WEAPON
- Q: SWITCH WEAPON
- H: USE FIRST AID KIT

THE ZOMBIES OF ZOMBOTRON ARE OUT TO EAT EVERYTHING THAT MOVES!

AWARDS

Gold
Rid Zombotron of all evil zombies and gain 60,000 points.

Silver
Complete the mission with a score of 40,000 points.

Bronze
Clean the planet of zombies and collect 25,000 points.

Alien Flagship Award
You are in total command! Score 15,000 points to win the Alien Flagship Award!

JOUSTING

JANE'S FAVE

THIS GAME ROCKS BECAUSE ...

Mount your medieval horse and prepare your lance, because it's time to head to a classic jousting tournament to defeat the bravest and meanest knights around. Your steed is trusty, but the aim and strength of the strike is all up to you. Only the brave and fortunate will live to tell the tale of the day they played Jousting on Miniclip!

IT'S TEMPTING TO STRIKE EARLY, BUT IF YOU MISS, YOU'RE A SITTING DUCK!

HIGH SCORE

16,700

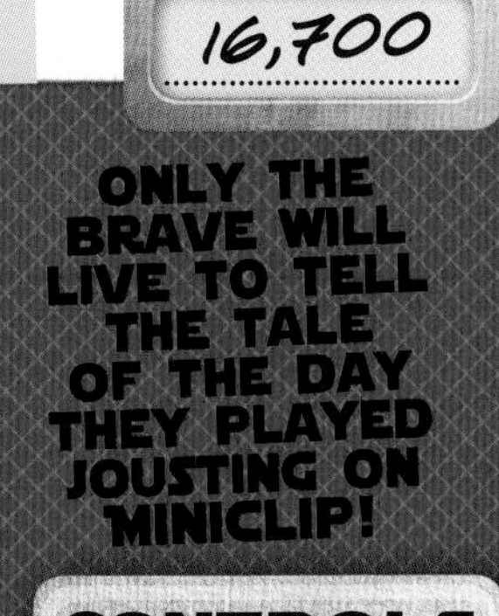

ONLY THE BRAVE WILL LIVE TO TELL THE TALE OF THE DAY THEY PLAYED JOUSTING ON MINICLIP!

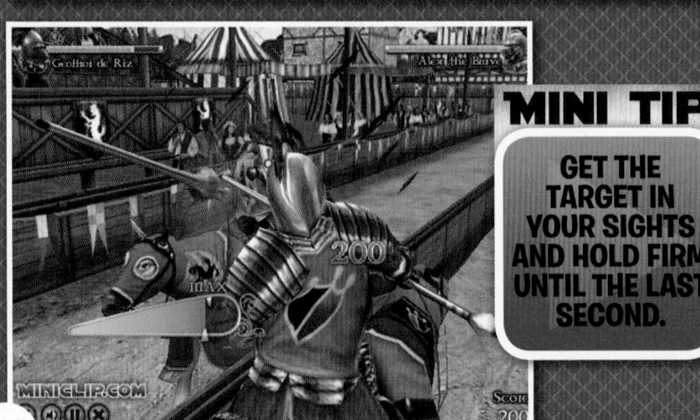

MINI TIP

GET THE TARGET IN YOUR SIGHTS AND HOLD FIRM UNTIL THE LAST SECOND.

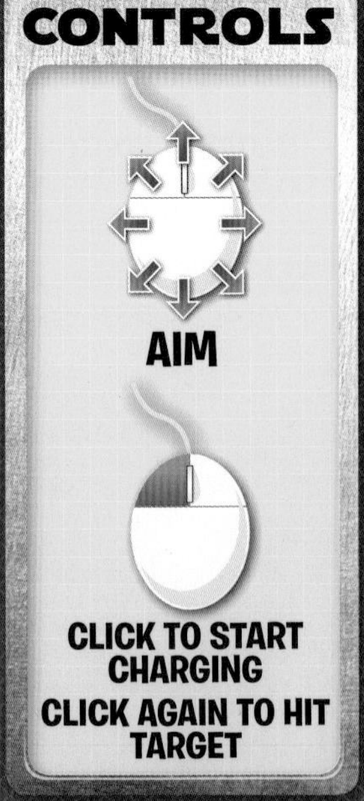

DISC POOL

BEN'S FAVE

THIS GAME ROCKS BECAUSE ...

It's pool, but not as we know it! Go up against live Miniclip players to become the ultimate Disc Pool champion. If you're not up for the challenge then take in some practice time. Chalk up your cue and pocket the discs.

HIGH SCORE

RANK 438

AWARDS

DISC POOL SCHOOL GOLD
Complete level 200 to get the Disc Pool School Gold award.

CHALK YOUR CUE AND POCKET THE DISCS.

CONTROLS

AIM

PRESS AND HOLD TO SHOOT

ALEXANDER'S FAVE

THIS GAME ROCKS BECAUSE ...

If you don't know the first thing about Club Penguin, then this is it in a nutshell. You can chat with other online penguins, dance, walk around, throw snowballs at each other and play games. By playing these games, you'll earn virtual coins to spend on clothing and fun accessories for your penguin and furniture for your igloo. So, let's join this ice-cool club!

IF YOU FANCY BEING A PENGUIN, THEN COME AND JOIN THE CLUB!

YOU CAN BE WHATEVER PENGUIN YOU WANT IN THE WORLD OF CLUB PENGUIN!

MINI TIP

THIS IS ONE OF THE BEST SOCIAL GAMING SITES OUT THERE, SO IT'S WELL WORTH CHECKING IT OUT.

CONTROLS

SELECT A PLACE TO MOVE TO

AMAZING SHERIFF
MINICLIP.COM
Amazing SHERIFF
Credits
Play More Games
Scores
Play
Your Best score is $ 24290
THERESE'S FAVE
THIS GAME ROCKS BECAUSE ...
Fasten on your new sheriff's badge and head for the Old West. However, here you're not patrolling ghost towns or dusty streets ... you're leaping from rotating cogs! Jump safely from one to the next collecting as much gold and smashing through as many bottles as you can. Oh yeah, and remember to get those pesky aliens!
RACK UP ONE COMBO AFTER ANOTHER AND WATCH YOUR SCORE ROCKET!
HIGH SCORE
52,850
$ 5360
0 Combo
$ 0
Help
click
Space
Double Jump
0 Combo
THIS COG AIN'T BIG ENOUGH FOR THE TWO OF US!
MINI TIP
THE CIRCULAR ALIENS ARE WORTH $100, SO MAKE SURE YOU HIT THOSE TO BOOST YOUR TOTAL.
$ 6210
+10
+10
+100
23 Combo
CONTROLS
JUMP

UFO JOE

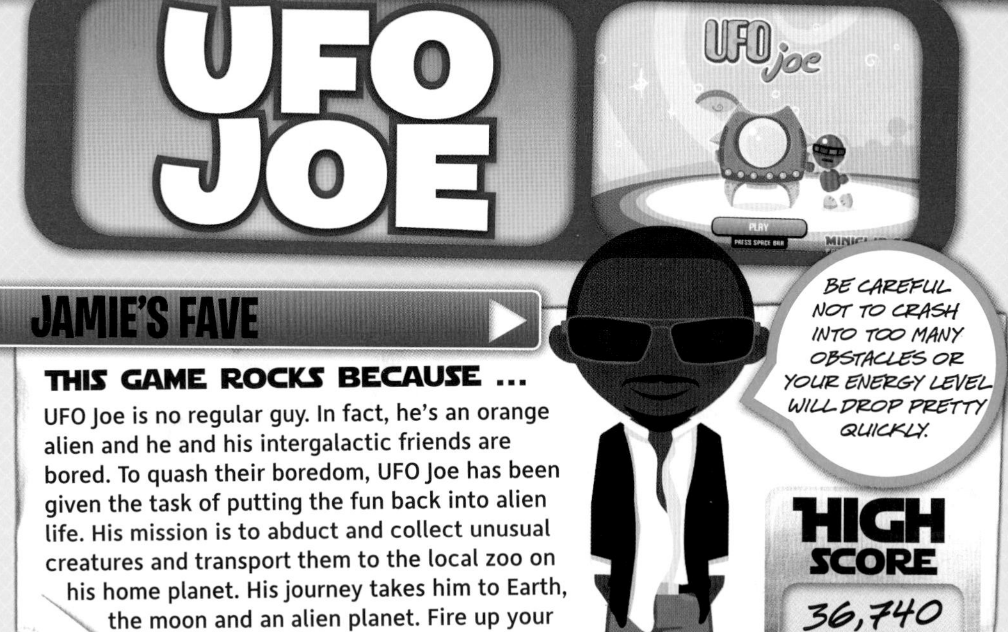

JAMIE'S FAVE

THIS GAME ROCKS BECAUSE ...

UFO Joe is no regular guy. In fact, he's an orange alien and he and his intergalactic friends are bored. To quash their boredom, UFO Joe has been given the task of putting the fun back into alien life. His mission is to abduct and collect unusual creatures and transport them to the local zoo on his home planet. His journey takes him to Earth, the moon and an alien planet. Fire up your tractor beam and blast off!

HIGH SCORE

36,740

ABDUCT AND COLLECT WEIRD CREATURES FOR THE ALIEN ZOO!

MINI TIP

YOUR FUEL IS LIMITED SO MOVE QUICKLY TO ABDUCT THOSE CREATURES.

CONTROLS

STEER

THRUST

SPACE

ACTIVATE TRACTOR BEAM

AWARDS

GOLD

Earn 18,000 points in order to fly the Golden Spaceship!

FRAGGER LOST CITY™

ROB L.'S FAVE

THIS GAME ROCKS BECAUSE...

This game is literally packed with explosive action. You have grenades and it's your job to aim, throw and wait for the detonation. It's you against the enemy, so take them out as precisely as you can. There's no time limit, so this game is all about skill and aim. It's time to wipe the smile off these crazy villains' faces!

AS YOU PROGRESS, HONE YOUR AIM. YOU'LL NEED TO THROW THOSE GRENADES THROUGH TUNNELS AND INTO PITS.

HIGH SCORE

125,245

CONTROLS

AIM AND SET POWER

FIRE GRENADE

SPACE

CANCEL A THROWN GRENADE

E

RETRY LEVEL

PREPARE FOR EXPLOSIVE ACTION AND DEFEAT THE ENEMY.

MINI TIP

YOU CAN'T BE DESTROYED, EVEN IF THE GRENADE ENDS UP BETWEEN YOUR LEGS. PHEW!

THIS GAME IS PACKED WITH EXPLOSIVE ACTION!

GAMES IN THE SERIES

FRAGGER

It's classic Fragger, with enemies ready to be obliterated! Plus, there's dancing clouds in this version!

FRAGGER BONUS BLAST

It's Fragger, but with an awesome Bonus Blast feature. Get blasting!

YOUR TIPS

So, you've heard all the tips from the experts, the developers and the madcap gang that make up Team Miniclip, but we wanted to hear from YOU! Here is a selection of favourite games and mega tips from Miniclip users all over the globe.

KCOOL1234

FAVOURITE GAMES:
Any Nitrome game, but **Square Meal** is my favourite. I like it because it's so cute and you can play with a friend, and it's just so awesome!

MY MEGA TIP:
I play all the time and whenever I can, so my advice to you is to always play!

KING-OLE

FAVOURITE GAMES:
Stunt Driver - Love driving games, and this one is just awesome.

MY MEGA TIP:
Be patient. Take your time to learn and adjust to a game. Join the forum and find/discuss game strategies and hints. Don't be afraid to ask. There will always be someone willing to help you improve.

LOOP8382

FAVOURITE GAMES:
I enjoy playing fun, quick games such as **Epic Coaster**, **Volcanic Airways** and **Flomo**. I also like platform games such as **Mimelet** and **Snow Drift**. Other games I like are **Pixel Cricket**, **China 2008** and my all time favourite in the site, **Stunt Dive**.

MY MEGA TIP:
Practise, practise, practise! Pick a game you enjoy playing and don't stop until you're satisfied with the result.

JESS118005

FAVOURITE GAMES:
I like **Love's Arrow**, **Mushroom Madness** and **Superhero Pizza** because my hand-eye coordination improves when I play those games.

MY MEGA TIP:

Try out each game repeatedly, check out the different aspects and levels of each game, interact with other game enthusiasts whenever a good opportunity presents itself, have fun!

TH100

FAVOURITE GAMES:
I like **Monkey Kick Off**, because it's a game that requires skill to conquer.

MY MEGA TIP:

Keep trying to get those high scores, no matter how much you fail. The secret in life is to fall seven times, then get up eight; every time you fail, you're bound to learn something.

THERESAL7

FAVOURITE GAMES:
8 ball multiplayer - I'm addicted! I like it because it's competitive.

MY MEGA TIP:

Take your time, nobody gets good overnight! Practise as much as you can to try and beat some of the top online opponents from around the world.

ARCTICFOX789

FAVOURITE GAMES:
UFO Joe - So entertaining. A game about an alien whose fellow aliens want you to collect Cows, Sheep, Spacemen and Aliens for their zoo. Basically, you have to get to the other landing pads on the level, if you are confident enough you can try and abduct the creatures on the level.

MY MEGA TIP:

There are 15 levels, but every time you die you have to start again from Level 1. It's great fun and you will get addicted to the game. You don't need to abduct but if you do - and do it carefully - you'll score 30,000-50,000 points.

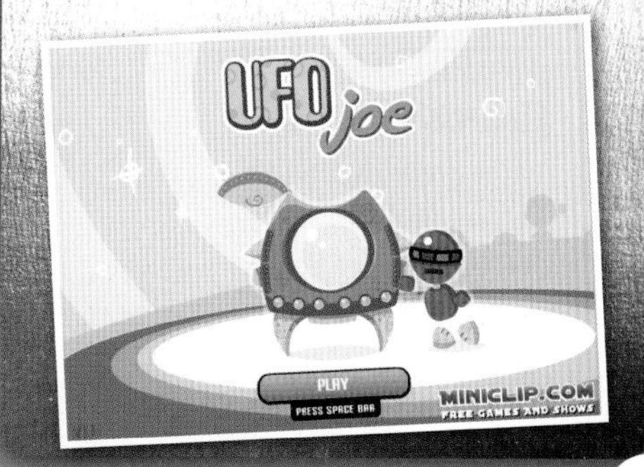

DEVELOPER Q&A

Name: Jan Rigerl
Age: 29
Lives: Malta

What's the hardest thing about game development?

Knowing if a game idea is good or not before investing all the time needed to create it.

What's your favourite game of all time?

Probably XCOM, the first one from '93. I've played it countless hours. Very much looking forward to the remake which is supposed to be released in 2012.

How many people in your team/studio? What do they do?

It's just me and my cat. I do the technical stuff and graphics and for some games I hire help with the graphics and sound. My cat does most of the eating and sleeping.

What advice would you give someone who wanted to work in games?

Stop thinking about it and start doing it. Be prepared for the fact that your first games are not likely to be masterpieces. Work samples are a great way to get a job.

What's your prediction for the future of games?

It's a growing market. I think more of it will move online, and actually buying games in physical stores is likely to go away.

Tell us a secret.

A lot of good game elements originate from mistakes.

What game are you most proud of?

I would say R.I.F.T., it's a platform puzzle game available on Miniclip.

Name: Jonathan Bartram
Age: 41
Lives: UK

How did you get started in game development?

A long time ago (1984), in my bedroom on a then-new Atari 800xl computer. My first game involved two cowboys shooting each other across the screen.

What's the hardest thing about it?

Coming up with fresh ideas and trying not to play games when you should be working.

What game are you most proud of?

My Penguins Attack series of games.

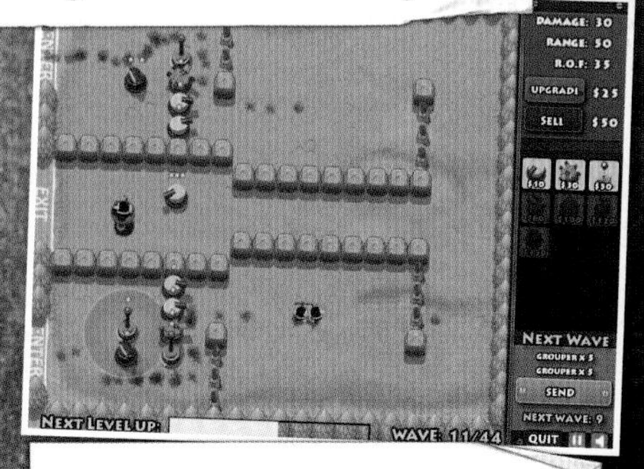

What's your favourite game on Miniclip (not made by you)?

It would have to be the Commando series of games. I remember when you had to head off to the arcades with a pocket full of change to have that much fun.

Where do you get your ideas for games?

Everywhere! My Penguins Attack game was originally inspired by a performance at my daughter's school ... there was a song about penguins with a military backing!

YOUR GAMING JOURNAL

Hey! Remember, this is YOUR book so here's a great chance to write down all your favourite things about the Miniclip universe. Why not ask to take a look at your friend's book and see how your notes compare?

MY FAVOURITE THING ABOUT MINICLIP IS ...

....

....

MY GOALS ON MINICLIP ARE ...

MY FAVOURITE JOB AT MINICLIP WOULD BE ...

....

BECAUSE ...
....

....

....

....

....

....

MY HIGHEST SCORE EVER ...

GAME: ....

SCORE: ....

MY TOP 10 MINICLIP GAMES ...

1 ....
2 ....
3 ....
4 ....
5 ....
6 ....
7 ....
8 ....
9 ....
10 ....

OTHER STUFF I LOVE ABOUT MINICLIP IS ...

IF I WERE TO DEVELOP A GAME IT WOULD BE ...

....

....

....

....

....

....

....

MY FAVE GAMES CATEGORY IS ...

NOTES:

FRIENDS ON MINICLIP:

....

....

....

....

GAMES A-Z

#
3 Foot Ninja
3 Foot Ninja II
5 in a Row
5 in a Row Gomoku
5 Min Shoot em Up
7 Dragons
8 Ball Pool Multiplayer
8 Ball Pool QFP
9 Ball Pool QFP
A
Acid Factory
Acno's Energizer
Adrenaline Bundle
Adventure Elf
Adventures of Bloo
Age Of Speed
Age of Speed 2
Agent Freeride
Agent Freeride 2
Agent: Freeride Aqua Escape
Agent P Strikes Back
Air Barons
Air Show
Alex in Danger
Alien Abduction
Alien Attack
Alien Clones
Alien Disorder
Alien Hive
Aliens Must Die
All Out
All We Need is Brain 2
Alphattack
Amazing Sheriff
American Football
Anagram Magic
Anagrammatic
Anika's Odyssey
Apache Overkill
Aqua Energizer
Aquanaut
Arctic Drift
Arcuz
Area Zero
Armada Tanks
Art Thief
Ask Guru Joe
Assault Course
Asteroid Rush
Avalanche
Awesome Tanks
Axon
B
Baby Blimp
Backfire
Bad Apple
Badaboom
Baja Motocross
Balance
Bank Robber
Base Jumper
Base Jumping
Baseball
Basketball Slam
Bazooki
Bears & Bees
Beat The Wall
Bee Boxing
Big Catch
Big Jump Challenge
Big Snow Tricks
Bionic Bugz
Black Knight
Blackjack Elf
Blair The Motivator
Blobs
Blobs 2
Block Drop
Bloomin' Gardens
Blox Forever
Bloxorz
Blues Bikers
BMX Freestyle
Bomba
Boom Bugs
Boom Volleyball
Bow Master
Boxing Bonanza
Boxo
BP Gas Mania
BP Rally
Brainwave
Bubble Trouble
Buck Ride
Bug On A Wire
Bullethead
Bullfrog Poker
Bullseye
Bunch
Bush Aerobics
Bush Shoot-Out
C
Cab Driver
Cable Capers 2
Cactus McCoy
Cactus McCoy 2
Canary
Candy and Clyde
Candy Magic
Cannon Blast
Canyon Defense
Canyon Defense 2
Canyon Glider
Canyon Shooter
Canyon Shooter 2
Car Chaos
Caravan Racers
Carnival Jackpot
Castle Conquest
Castle Corp
Catapult
Cave Chaos
Cave of Despair
Caveman
Celeb Table Tennis
Cell Out
Chasm
Cheese Dreams
Cherie 'Disco' Blair
Chick Flick
China 2008
Chisel
Christmas Balls
Christmas Mayhem
Chronotron
ChuckaBOOM
Civilization wars
Clash N Slash
Classroom Pilot
Click & Slide
ClickPLAY
Clone Wars
Clowning Around
Club Penguin
Coign of Vantage
Cold Storage
Commander n Chief
Commando
Commando 2
Commando 2 Trailer
Commando 3
Commando Assault
Commando Defense
Couronne Deluxe
Cowabunga Candace
Cranergy Ball
Crash Car Combat
Crash Football
Crashdown
Crazy Go Nuts 2
Crazy Karts
Creepy Pong
Cricket Defend the Wicket
Crimson Viper
Crossword Daily
Crush the Castle 2
Crypt Raider
Cube Buster
Cursed Treasure
Cursor Chaos
Cyber Mice Party
D
Da Numba
Dale and Peakot
Dance 2 the Beat
Dance Planet
Dancing Blair
Dancing Bush
Dancing Hillary
Dancing Palin
David
DecaJump
Deep Freeze
Deep Sea Patrol
Defenders
Deluxe Pool
Desert Ambush
Detonator
Digital Switch
Dino Quake
Dino Run
Dirk Valentine
Disc Golf
Disc Pool
Doeo
Dogfight
Dojo Dodge
Doodle
Doodle 2
Down Hill Chill
Down Perryscope
DownWorld
Dr Compactor
Dragon Attack
Dream Racer
Dream Tower
Droid Retaliation
Drumming Alchemist
Dune Buggy
E
Egg Blast
Egg Run
Egyptian Tale
Elastic Soccer
Electro Air Hockey
Elements and Magic
Elfquilibrium
Empty Santa's Sack
European Soccer Champions
Evac
Exile
Extreme Pamplona
Extreme Quad
Extreme Skater
Extreme Trial
Extreme Triathlon
F
FA-18
Family Barn
Fancy Pants 1
Fancy Pants 2
Fantage
Farmer
Fast Car Frenzy
Fat Cat
Fat Slice
Feather Keeper
Feed Me
Field Goal
Fighter Patrol 42
Fighter Pilot
Fighter Pilot 2
Filler
Final Fortress
Final Ninja
Final Ninja Zero
Finders Keepers
Fire Storm
Fireworks
Flavor Fling
Fling
Flingo
Flip Words
Flomo
Fly Guy
Forest Temple
Forks and Arrows
Formula G1
Formula Racing
Fowl Words
Fowl Words 2
Fragger
Fragger Bonus
Fragger Lost City
Frantic
Fred Figglehorn
Free Aqua Zoo
Free Kick Challenge
Free Realms
Free Running
Free Wheels
Freestyle Snowboard
Frendz
Fresh Water Bounce
Frost Bite
Frost Bite 2
Fruit Smash
FunGoPlay
Funky Nurse
G
Gadget Golf
Galactic Goobers
Galactic Warrior
Galaxy Gunner
Gamma Bros
Garden Gnome
Carnage
Gas & Sand
Gateway
Gemaica
Ghostfire Attack
Ghosts Stole My Dog
Gift Keeper
Gingerbread Circus
Gladiators
Glassworks
Gnomeo Kart
Go Karts
Go Santa Go
Goal Keeper
Golf Ace
Golf Ace Hawaii
Golf Solitaire
Golfish
Goodgame Empire
Goodgame Mafia
Governor of Poker
Governor of Poker 2
Granny Strikes Back
Graveyard Shift
Gravinaytor
Gravity
Gravity Guy
Gripz Globe Skater
Groundhog D-day
Gun Run
Gyroball
H
Habbo Hotel
Hambo
Hangaroo
Hangaroo 2
Harvey Wallbanger
Haunted House
Heart Breaker
Heli Attack 2
Heli Attack 3
Hen Coops
Hexxagon
Hill Billy Flea
Hip-Hop Debate
Hive Hero
Hockey Showdown
Hong Kong Ninja
Horsey Racing
Hostile Skies
Hot Air
Hot Air 2
Hot Rods
Hotel Skeleton
Hunter
I
Ice Breaker
Ice Breaker RC
Ice Breakout
Ice Racer
Ice Slide
Ice Temple
Icy Slicy
In The Doghouse
Insane Ski Jump
iStunt 2
J
Jet Ski
Jet Ski Racing
Jet Velocity
Jet Velocity 2
Jigsaw - Car
Jigsaw - Ocean
Jingo
Joe Destructo
Jousting
Jump Start
K
K Million
Karate King
Kerry Workout
Kickboxing
Kindergarten
King of the Hill
KingPin Bowling
Klondike Solitaire
Kraft Lunchables
Kung Fu Statesmen
L
Lamb Chop Drop
Last Christmas 2
Lavalab
LEGO: Make the Game
Leo Steel
Letter Lasso
Letter Rip
Light Heroes
Light Temple
Little Dancer Cont
Little Fins
Little Wheel
Loco Launcho
Lorax
Love's Arrow
Lumberjack Games
Lunar Command
M
Magic Balls
Magic Pen
Magic Pen 2
Mahjong Daily
Maldark
Mallet Mania
Mars Patrol
Masters of Wrestling
Math Blaster
Max Speed
Meez

Merlin's Christmas
Merry Christmas
Michael Jackson
Migo Land
Milk Shake
Mimelet
Mini Golf
Mini Soccer
Miniclip Baseball
Miniclip Free Bike
Miniclip Rally
Minilympics
MiniMonos
Mining Truck
Mining Truck 2
Mini Pets
Mission Mars
Mister Easter
Moby Dick
Moby Dick 2
Monkey Kick Off
Monkey Lander
Monkey Mines
Monkey Quest
Monkey Snowfight
Monster Bash
Monster Basher
Monster Castle
Monster Golf
Monster Invasion
Monster Island
Monster Mowdown 2
Monster Sumo
Monster Trucks
Monster Trucks Nitro
Monster Trucks Nitro 2
Moon Rush
Moonshadow
Most Wanted
MotherLoad
Moto Trial Fest
Motocross Country Fever
Motocross Fever
Motocross Urban
Mountain Bike
Movie Munchies
Mr Bounce
Mr Men Pinball
Mushroom Madness
Mushroom Madness 3
Music Cube

N

Nano Recon
Nat Geo Animal Jam
Need for Madness
Neon Race
Ninja Dogs 2
Ninja Glove
Ninja Painter
Ninja Pig
Nordic Chill
Notepad Chaos
Nuclear Zombie 2000
Numbskull

O

Obama Alien Defense
Off The Rails
Offroad 4x4
On The Run
On The Run 2
On The Run Vegas
One and One Story
One Man Band
Onekey
OurWorld
Outpost Swarm
Overkill Apache

P

Paintball
Panfu
Panik in Chocoland
Papa Louie
Park a Lot
Park a Lot 2
Peanut
Pearl Diver
Pebble Dash
Pencak Silat
Pengapop
Pengu Wars
Penguin Arcade
Penguin Push
Penguin Pusher
Penguin Rush
Pest Control
Petpet Park
Pets vs Monsters
Pharaoh's Tomb
Ping Pong
Pipe Riders
Pipsoh!
Piranhas
Pirate Chains
Pirate Golf
Pixel Cricket
Pixie Hollow
Pizza Hot
Planet Cruncher
Plant Pong
Pod Panic
Polar Dash
Polar Jump
Polar Rescue
Police Chopper
Police Pursuit
Pop Pirates
Power Boat
Power Soccer
Present Panic
Presidential Paint
Presidential Pound
Pro Football
Pumpkin Push
Puzzle Pirates

Q

QuickHit NFL

R

R.I.F.T.
Raceway 500
Radical Aces
Raft Wars
Railroad Rampage
Rails of War
Rango
Rapid Wars
RC Time Trial
Real Space 2
Red Beard
Red Bugs Puzzle
Red Code 3
Red Cross ERU
Red Riot
Reel Gold
Reindeer Bounce
Retroshoot 360
Rhino Rush
Rich Racer
Rifleman
Rigelian Hotshots
Ringshot
Rival Rage
River Raider
Rizk
ROBLOX
Robo Pop
Robo Rampage
RoboKill
Robot Shooting
Rocketman
Rockitty
Rodeo Ride-off
Rollercoaster
Rolley
Rollo and Flex
RollOn
Roly Poly
Rooftop-Hop
Royal Rampage
Royal Wedding
Rubble Trouble
Rubble Trouble Moscow
Rubble Trouble Tokyo
Rugby Challenge
Rule The Beach
Run N Gun
Run The Rapids
RuneScape
Rural Racer

S

Saloon Brawl
Samurai Defense
Samurai Sam
Samurai Warrior
Sandman
Sandstorm
Santa Balls 2
Santa Ski Jump
Santa's Cannon
Santa's Gift Jump
Save the Fallen
Save the Sheriff
Scraper Caper
Scribble
Sewer Run
Shadow Factory
Shadows of Mummies
Shanghai Mahjongg
Shark Bait
Sheep Game
Sheepish
Sheriff Tripeaks
Shift 2
Shootin' Hoops
Shopping Mall Parking
Short History of the World
Shove It
Show Jumping
Shrunken Heads
Siege Hero
Silversphere
Simon Says
Simple Soccer
Skateboard Jam
Sketch Star
Ski Run
Skies of War
Sky Golf
Skyboard
Skywire
Skywire 2
Slacking
Sleigh Shot
Slime Laboratory
Sling
Slingfire
Slingshot
Small Fry
Smashing
Smokin' Barrels
Snake
Snap n Spooky
Sneeze
Sniper
Snow Day
Snow Drift
Snow Fight
Snow Line
Snow Line 2
Snow Riders
Snow Tale
Snowball
Snowball Warfare
Snowboard Madness
Snowboarder XS
Snowbowl
Snowman Stacker
Snowman's Hat
Snowmen Parade
Soap Bubble
Soap Bubble 2
Soccer Five
Soccer Games
Soccer Pro
Soccer Stars
Space Escape
Space Fighter
Space Hopper
Spark City World
Spectral Wizard
Spider Game
Spiral Knights
Sportbike Sprint
SQRL Golf
SQRL Golf 2
Square Meal
Squiggle Squid
Stackopolis
Stan Skates
Starship Eleven
Starship Gunner
Starship Seven
Stay the Distance
Storybook
Street Fight
Street Luge
Stunt Crazy
Stunt Dive
Stunt Driver
Stunt Pilot
Stunt Pilot 2
Stuntman
Sub Commander
Sudoku
Sugar Sugar Xmas
Summer Athletics
Super Goblin War Machine
Super Robot War
Super Trucks
Superbike GP
Superbike Race Off
SuperCyclone
Superhero Pizza
Superstar Racing
Superstar Streetz
Surf's Up
Surfmania
Sushi Cat
Sushi Go Round
Sveerz

T

Trick or Treat Smash
T.A.N.K.S
Table Tennis
Table Tennis
Tabletop Cricket
Tank Attack
Tanked Up
Tanki Online
Tarnation
Tennis Ace
Tennis Doubles
Tennis Grand Slam
Tennis Titans
TGMotocross 3
The Ashes
The Godfather
The Scruffs
Thin Ice
Thrill Coaster
Thunder Plunder
Tiger Golf
Tiny Castle
Toboggan Run
Tooth N Claw
Top Cop
Topsy Turvy
Toys vs Nightmares
Traps, Mines, Sheep
Trapshoot
Trech
Trech 2
Trial Bike
Trial Bike Bundle
Trial Bike Pro
Trials 2
Trials Construction
Trials Dynamite
Trials Mountain Heights
Tribe
TriPeaks Solitaire
Trivia Machine
Tron
Tropi Golf
Troy
Tumblestump 2
Turbo Racing
Turbo Racing 2
Turkey Run
Twiddlestix
Twisted City

U

UFO Joe
United We Dance
Up Beat
Urban Basketball

V

Vector Rush
Vectoroids
Verti Golf
Verti Golf 2
Viking Defense
Viper
Volcanic Airways
Vuvuzela

W

Wacky Ballz
Waffle Mania
Wait 4 Me
Wakeboard Pro
Wakeboarding XS
War Copter
War of Legends
Wave Jumper
Webosaurs
Weirdville
Whack a Ground Hog
Wheels of Salvation
White Water Rafting
Winter Bow Master
Winter Games
Winter Workout
Wizard Hult
Wizard101
Wonderputt
Wood Runner
Word Collapse
Word Sailing
Word Vine
Wordo
World Cricket 2011
World Domination 2
World Rugby 2011
World Soccer
World Soccer Champ
Worm Food
Wrap Attack

X

Xbox Party Mansion
XRaye

Y

YoMe Creator
Youda Camper
Youda Farmer 2
Youda Legend
Youda Marina
Youda Safari
Youda Survivor
Youda Sushi Chef

Z

Zed
Zoikz
Zoikz 2
Zombie Crypt
Zombie Defense Agency
Zombie Dolls
Zombie Stalker
Zombotron
Zoo Racer
Zubo Zurfing

usama
Muhammad
Saadk23
7Chocolate
Agent Steve
The-Gimi36
JokerBoy8
Mladipravnik
Eren5534
m4rt1n
Janus
waleedmumtaz
Cheeseymonster
DJ Wrapper
hermioneandron7
ArcticFox789
scarlet0102
timestrike
M4 IV
Strictlyfan2010
Nana
Ckgummi
Buddy Sutt
Shadowman1111
Raisynbrangurl
Ali
Wooster8988
American Girl
theresal7
Paolo